CAMBRIDGE IGCSE® ICT

Revision Guide

Colin Stobart

ACKNOWLEDGEMENTS
Cover photo: DreamLand Media / Shutterstock
Illustrations by QBS and Ann Paganuzzi
Images p8: Zern Liew/Shutterstock, Luisa Leal Photography/Shutterstock, Ksander/Shutterstock, You can more/Shutterstock; page 9: Bagiuiani/Shutterstock, Oleksandr Molotkovych/Shutterstock, Nucleartist/Shutterstock, page 38: StockLite/Shutterstock
Supplementary images for download: Colin Stobart

Every effort has been made to trace copyright holders and obtain their permission for the use of copyright material. The author and publisher will gladly receive information enabling them to rectify any error or omission in subsequent editions. All facts are correct at time of going to press.

Published by Letts Educational
An imprint of HarperCollinsPublishers
The News Building
1 London Bridge Street
London
SE1 9GF

ISBN 978-0-00-821037-3

First published 2017

10 9 8 7 6 5 4 3 2 1

® IGCSE is the registered trademark of Cambridge International Examinations.
All exam-style questions, related example answers given on the website, marks awarded and comments that appear in this book were written by the author. In examinations, the way marks are awarded to questions and answers like these may be different.

Colin Stobart asserts his moral right to be identified as the author of this work.

British Library Cataloguing in Publication Data
A CIP record for this book is available from the British Library.

Commissioned by Katherine Wilkinson
Project managed by Kate Ellis, Sheena Shanks
Edited by Helen Bleck
Proofread by Louise Robb
Cover design by Paul Oates
Typesetting by QBS
Production by Natalia Rebow, Lyndsey Rogers and Paul Harding
Printed and bound in the UK

FSC™ is a non-profit international organisation established to promote the responsible management of the world's forests. Products carrying the FSC label are independently certified to assure consumers that they come from forests that are managed to meet the social, economic and ecological needs of present and future generations, and other controlled sources.

Find out more about HarperCollins and the environment at
www.harpercollins.co.uk/green

Contents

Introduction

This revision guide is designed to support your studies for the Cambridge IGCSE in ICT. It contains content linked to the syllabus, provides revision tips, theory questions and practical activities designed to prepare you for the three examinations.

However, it is important to remember that this is a revision guide. It has a similar structure to the Collins Cambridge IGCSE ICT Student Book and contains everything you need to know, but it does not contain the depth and detail you might get from your own notes or from the textbook. It is therefore a good idea to use this book as one of the tools to prepare you for the exam, but it should not necessarily be the only tool in your toolkit.

The content of this book is split into 13 units. The first eight cover each of the eight theory units in the syllabus and the remaining five cover each of the five practical elements that are examined.

At the end of each chapter within a unit there is a 'true or false' quick test to check that you have understood the main aspects of the topic area, and at the end of each unit there is a series of examination-style questions which are reflective of the type and style of questions you will get in the exam. The answers to all the quick tests and the longer examination-style questions are in the back of the book.

For the practical units you will need a number of pre-prepared files to enable you to complete the chapter exercises and end of unit exam-style questions. These can be downloaded from the revision guide support webpage: www.collins.co.uk/IGCSEICTrevision; it is a good idea to visit the page and download all the files in one visit rather than keep going back to the webpage as you begin each new exercise.

The answers and sample solutions to all the practical questions can also be downloaded from the support webpage and you will also find help and advice about how to prepare for each of the three examinations.

When you are reading through the chapters you will notice that on each page several of the words are in **bold**. These are key terms you will need to learn and be able to use. The definitions for these words can be found in the glossary at the back of the book, making it easy to find the meanings of the key words that you need.

Revision tips appear in each chapter. These might suggest an additional activity such as researching or investigating a particular aspect of the course in preparation for the examination. They might also highlight particular concepts that students typically get confused about.

Finally, have a think about how you revise. While you may want to focus on your own learning, it is always a good idea to meet up with other ICT students and, for at least some of the time, revise together. You can help each other with aspects of the course that one of you might not understand, and devise quizzes to test each other. Working with friends can also prove very useful when tackling the practical parts of your revision, since we all have quick tips and practices that help us in our own work. Most importantly, revision with someone else is usually more productive and fun than when you revise on your own.

If you work your way carefully through the materials presented in this book you will be well prepared.

Good luck.

Help to prepare for examination

The theory paper

There will be questions covering the whole syllabus, so be prepared to answer questions about anything on the syllabus.

Command words

There are a number of words and phrases to look out for across the paper. These could be called key words or command words.

Key word/example use	Advice on how to respond
Name the methods of storage …	One-word answers or a list.
Give two reasons …	A short sentence, not just a one-word answer.
Explain why a laser printer was chosen …	At least one full sentence will be needed that also gives some specific and qualifying information.
Describe four advantages …	Give full-sentence answers. If you are asked for a number of advantages, each one must be significantly different from another.
Discuss the advantages and disadvantages …	Requires a free-form answer, a lengthy paragraph rather than a numbered sequence of separate answers. Present a balanced answer, both sides of the debate, in properly constructed paragraphs, including a conclusion – avoid bulleted lists, except in preparing your answer.

The practical papers

The second paper assesses your practical skills using word processing, database and presentation software (syllabus sections 17, 18 and 19) and may draw on other generic skills from sections 11 to 16.

The third paper assesses your practical skills using spreadsheet and web authoring software (syllabus sections 20 and 21) and may also draw on other generic skills from sections 11 to 16.

You may also be asked theory questions within some parts of the practical examination. For example, the answer to a question may need to be added in a text box on a presentation slide, or an analysis of some element of a style sheet may need to be included in your evidence document.

Webpage   Path names are vitally important. They should always be relative and not absolute. When these files are placed or referenced the file pathname should only be **folder\filename** and not something like **c\\:my documents\exam stuff\exam\web\cieweb\filename**. The reason for this is that if your webpage (and supporting files) were uploaded to a server, the references to images and stylesheets should point to the files on the server (relative) and not your home computer hard drive (absolute).

Document production Check that you have the right page orientation and if you have changed the page orientation check the alignment of any headers and footers you are using. This is especially important if you change from landscape to portrait. At the end of the examination, check for consistency in spacing, that there are no widows or orphans and for spelling and grammar.

Data analysis Check for the printout being either formula or data sheet view. The examiner is looking at your use of formulae and functions – not the values that are displayed. You will always lose a number of marks if the whole formulae are not visible, so resize the column widths to make sure they are.

Presentations Carefully read the information about how elements on the master slide are to be placed. Unless specified, make sure that no element overlaps or touches another.

Data manipulation Make sure that all fields are formatted correctly: currency and decimal places, Boolean and the correct states. Printing with an orientation of landscape means that more fields can be fitted across the page, but that might not always be the orientation that is required. Labels must always be fully visible. Be sure of what part of a page any run-time calculation should be placed into: detail, page, report.

In both practical papers be clear what you have to print. You will probably need a printout of, for example, a changed .css file, a browser printout of a webpage itself, a specific range of cells in a spreadsheet, presentation slides with notes, as well as your evidence document. Read through the question paper and use a highlighting pen to mark the exact requirements. Remember that you must have your name, candidate number and centre number printed on every page of printout that you submit. Any page that does not have these details, or does but handwritten, will not be marked.

Types of computer

Computer systems are classified according to size.

Type	Features/Use	Advantages/Disadvantages
Mainframe	Very large, used in organisations with vast amounts of data needing rapid processing: banks, travel, retail and manufacturing industries	Advantages: • very fast processing speeds • large memory • complex problem solving Disadvantages: • needs a lot of space • expensive maintenance • specialist staff
Desktop or **personal computer** (PC)	Small, general purpose, comprising: monitor, keyboard, mouse, processor and storage	Advantages: • standardised parts • faster processors than laptops Disadvantages: • lack of portability • files need to be copied to a removable storage device for transfer to another machine/location
Laptop or **notebook**	All components are within a single portable unit, allowing the computer to be used in different locations as required	Advantages: • small, portable • can be used anywhere, especially if WiFi can be accessed Disadvantages: • potential loss and theft • limited battery life • component upgrade is difficult
Tablet	Small, portable and all interaction with the user is through touch. Will run desktop/laptop applications but with reduced functionality. Exploits wireless technology to connect with other devices	Advantages: • portable, easy to use • uses flash memory so quick start-up • 3G and 4G technology allows fast internet and cloud access Disadvantages: • touch typing is difficult • WiFi access needed to exploit capabilities

Type	Features/Use	Advantages/Disadvantages
Personal Digital Assistant (PDA)	Small, handheld, has a touch screen and (often) a traditional keyboard. Has GPS and mobile phone capability and will run special versions of application software.	Advantages: • extremely portable • internet connectivity • designed for organising personal information Disadvantages: • with small keyboards, typing difficult • reduced functionality of applications
Smartphone	A small tablet computer with telephone capability. Combines the features of a PDA with web browsing and 1000s of applications.	Advantages: • online access to data • integrated apps such as camera, media players, social media Disadvantages: • similar size problems as PDA • some websites will look/ function differently to how they would on larger devices

Desktop and laptop computers, whether used in a business environment or at home, can be used as **stand-alone devices** or within a network. When you are the sole user of the computer, in control of the application working on the device, and the only user connected to other devices such as a printer, you are using the computer as a stand-alone device. When you are connected to other users and sharing resources such as a printer, storage space or the internet you are using a computer that is **networked**.

Revision tip

Make sure you can match a computer type to a typical situation/use/industry.

Hardware and software

Hardware forms the physical components of a computer system. In this picture can you identify the hardware components/devices: monitor (output), keyboard (input), mouse (input), speakers (output) and printer (output)? The tower also contains some hardware components such as memory chips, the motherboard, video and sound cards, as well as the internal hard disk drives. You will need to be able to identify these components.

Software is the programs, instructions and data that control the operation of the computer and is classified as one of two types: **system software** and **applications software**. A computer's operating system is the main item of system software but other examples are: device drivers, compilers, linkers, and utilities such as file management programs. Application software/programs help the user solve problems, and include word processors, spreadsheets, database and information management systems, control and measuring systems, applets and apps, photo-editing software, and video editing software.

Revision tip

Do not use product names when application software needs to be described: use 'word processor' and not 'Microsoft Word'.

Quick test

Are the following statements true or false?

A laptop computer can be networked	
The data held on a memory stick/flash drive is software	
A mainframe computer would be used by a family business run from home	
A desktop computer cannot be networked	
A memory stick is a piece of hardware	
Antivirus software is system software	

The main components of a computer system

The main components of any computer system are its processor and memory. Without a processor there would be no computer system. Inputted data needs to be processed.

If the covers of a computer, smartphone or any other device are taken off, the first item that is noticeable is the **motherboard** – the main circuit board holding all the crucial electronic components including the processor (CPU) and main memory.

The **Central Processing Unit** – (CPU) is a single integrated circuit at the centre of a system, interpreting and executing commands from the computer's hardware and software.

The computers identified on page 8 perform a wide variety of tasks and are general purpose computers – their processors are programmable. A **microprocessor** is a special form of CPU used in microcomputers and small computerised devices. When a microprocessor is built into a control device, such as a burglar alarm, it has been pre-programmed to only ever carry out that one task.

The **main memory** of a computer is connected directly to the CPU and is often referred to as central memory. There are two types of central memory:

- **Random Access Memory (RAM)** loses its contents when power is turned off. It is read/write memory and data is temporarily stored here when applications are running. Computers have increasingly large RAM capacity to speed up processing times.
- **Read Only Memory (ROM)** is permanent memory used to store instructions that the computer needs to go through when power is switched on such as **BIOS**, the **B**asic **I**nput and **O**utput **S**ystem, which checks all attached hardware devices are working properly and copies the operating system into RAM.

Storage devices, or **backing storage**, are used to store programs and data for later use when the computer is switched off. They are external to the computer and can be moved from computer to computer. Examples are portable hard drives, DVD-ROMs and flash memory cards. Most people carry important files on memory sticks and flash drives.

> **Revision tip**
>
> Make sure you can distinguish between the uses of main memory and backing storage.

Operating systems

Operating systems are system software that controls all **peripheral** devices, handles the running of application programs, maintaining the security of the system as well as managing the **user interface** that allows the user to interact with the computer system.

There are two main types of user interface: **Command Line Interface (CLI)** and **Graphical User Interface (GUI)**.

Command line interfaces allow the user to communicate directly with the computer by typing instructions and responding to prompts. This is a precise and quick method of control that does not require much memory, but the user does need to remember a number of commands and their syntax.

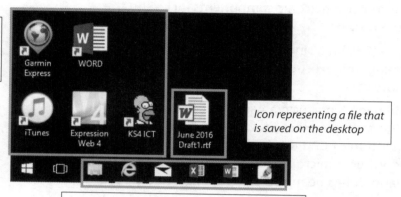

Command Prompt

```
H:\COS Files\Webs\PHP\Web logging>copy *.php "h:\cos files\webs\mikes"
logger.php
to add to each page for logging.php
        2 file(s) copied.

H:\COS Files\Webs\PHP\Web logging>_
```

A command to copy some files in one directory to another directory

Graphical user interfaces, such as a **WIMP** interface, use pictures and symbols (**icons**) to represent applications and files, which are selected or activated by using a pointing device such as a mouse or the user's finger. WIMP stands for **W**indow, **I**con, **M**enu, **P**ointing device.

Icons representing shortcuts to application software, and a directory (KS4 ICT)

Icon representing a file that is saved on the desktop

Icons representing applications that are currently running but whose windows are minimised because they are not being used right now

Quick test

Are the following statements true or false?

CLI are difficult to learn	
GUI is applications software	
Backing store devices are connected directly to the CPU	
RAM is used to store data permanently	
ROM retains data even when the power is switched off	
The microprocessor in a dishwasher can be reprogrammed	

The impact of emerging technologies

New innovation shifts the way technology is actually used, so what emerging technologies are starting to have an impact on our everyday life?

Artificial intelligence biometrics make use of the fact that some of our physical features (such as fingerprints, face, iris, voice) are unique to us and can therefore be used by security systems to identify us. Students' fingerprints are taken prior to taking an examination and then used to identify them at various stages of the examination such as between components which may happen over different days. Finger and palm print recognition technology may be used in door locks on cars as well as for entry to buildings.

Iris recognition devices already allow quick movement through airports, but could be used in many other locations where security is important. **Facial recognition systems** might also be used to enhance security.

Data security is increasingly important. **Cryptography** plays a vital role in keeping information such as credit card and bank account details secure when shopping online, as well as ensuring stolen data cannot be understood.

Robotics technology is not confined to manufacturing and space exploration, but has a place in many areas of everyday life. The current development of driverless cars illustrates this.

Text translation is no longer concerned with conversion of text from one language to another, starting afresh with each script. Databases of phrases, sentences and clauses of previously translated text are searched and added to with better or more accurate translations, and software builds translations from these.

3D printers are already having a tremendous impact in the medical field with the ability to 'print' heart valves, prosthetics limbs and even skin. Aid organisations working in poverty-stricken or war-ravaged areas can easily 3D print simple medical tools. You need to be able to outline some of the developments in these areas.

Other areas where advances in technology are driving new applications are **vision enhancement**, 3D imaging, **holography** and **virtual reality**. These have exciting potential in medicine, archaeology and travel – not just entertainment.

Mass media communication

Computers are used in the production of a wide variety of communication media, including:

- Newsletters, flyers and posters
- Websites
- Multimedia presentations
- Music scores
- Cartoons

Each of these is achieved by using application software designed specifically for the task. It is important that the purpose and audience for

> **Revision tip**
>
> Think of applications for these technologies: text translation for multilingual websites, robotics to clean up/search areas of a natural or industrial disaster, or 3D imaging or virtual reality in medicine.

> **Revision tip**
>
> Organisations usually have a corporate image, or house style, which determines the colours, fonts and other layout details that need to be used in all publicity such as business cards, letterheads and brochures.

these communications is understood because this helps to determine style and content.

For example, multimedia presentations engage the audience, often showing and explaining to them the content of a topic by using not just text, but images, charts and diagrams, sound, video and animation. The same is true of websites that are now so heavily interactive. Because of this audience need, the designers of any communication media have to fully analyse the purpose of the communication in order to ensure that the information communication is effective and relevant. If this is not done successfully the audience will not engage with the message and a marketing, sales or publicity opportunity is wasted.

It is also important to consider the audience that will be accessing these media solutions. Countries have differing views on what is morally and ethically acceptable, and freedom of speech, religious and sexual tolerance varies from country to country. What is acceptable for one audience may not be for another.

Effective, good-looking publicity materials such as newsletters, flyers and posters which contain text and images can be produced quickly and easily by using **word processing** and **desktop publishing** (DTP) software.

Essentially, websites are electronic versions of newsletters, flyers and posters. Webpages can be created in a simple text editor but to produce an effective, eye-catching webpage, **web authoring** software should be used. Video, sound and animation provide interest but it is also possible to add user interaction by providing a means of responding to what is seen: hyperlinks, response buttons, comments.

Multimedia presentations can be a very powerful communication tool. Audiences can be presented with information in many different forms with links to websites, videos and music. Presentations can be found in many diverse situations.

Application software for creating music scores and cartoons speeds up production with elements changed, enhanced, replayed and printed automatically. The quantity (and quality) of computer generated imagery (CGI) in films and TV has advanced dramatically in recent years.

> **Revision tip**
>
> It is important to be aware of the impact of music and animation software.

Quick test

Are the following statements true or false?

Iris recognition can be used on public transport	
Cryptography is necessary for social media posts	
DTP software can be used to produce advertising material	
Text can be translated word by word using an online dictionary	
A cartoon feature film can be completely computer-generated	
A person's weight is important AI biometric information	

Exam-style practice questions

1 Place a tick in the correct column to identify each item as hardware or software. [3 marks]

	Hardware	Software
Disk drive		
Spreadsheet		
RAM chip		
File manager		
Windows 10/Android		

2 Place a tick in the correct column to identify each item as application or system software.

	Application	System
Web browser		
File compression program		
Database		
File conversion program		
BIOS		

[3 marks]

3 Place a tick in the correct column to identify whether each item is a peripheral device or not.

	Yes	No
RAM		
Mouse		
Scanner		
Motherboard		
Printer		

[3 marks]

4 Outline one advantage and one disadvantage of using cloud storage. [2 marks]

5 State two differences between Random Access Memory and Read Only Memory. [2 marks]

6 Identify two common features of a tablet device and a smartphone. [2 marks]

7 Give two reasons why it is useful to store files on a memory stick or flash drive. [2 marks]

8 Describe the advantages to a travelling salesman of collecting and analysing data on a laptop computer rather than a tablet device. [2 marks]

9 Sara has bought a new washing machine which contains a microprocessor. She says that she can program the washing machine. Her husband says that this is not possible. Actually they are both right but for very different reasons. Why? [2 marks]

10. What is the difference between having a desktop computer that is a stand-alone device and one that is networked? [1 mark]

   Give an example use of each of these types. [2 marks]

11. Discuss why a bank would require a mainframe computer rather than a network of desktop computers. [4 marks]

12. An operating system is being created for a new tablet device for children. Explain why the developers should be considering a GUI rather than a CLI system. [3 marks]

13. Jonas says that he has stored his coursework project on his computer's ROM chip. Explain why this is not true. [2 marks]

14. You are applying for the position of Digital Director at a school which seeks to employ emerging technology in different areas of the school. The Principal of the school is particularly interested in developing systems in the dining hall and for pupil attendance. Identify and explain one idea for each of these two areas. [4 marks]

The data processing cycle:

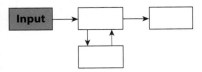

Input devices are used to get data into a computer system, where it is processed and output is produced. Data is all around us and needs to be collected somehow, meaning there are many input devices.

Data can be either digital or analogue. Computers process **digital data**, data that only comprises 0s and 1s (binary data). Some data is already digital, such as that entered via a keyboard or number pad. There are many other applications where the data to be captured is not digital. Data collected by sensors such as temperature or humidity, which might be used to control a greenhouse, or monitoring environmental/climate indicators or oxygen levels, for controlling the environment in a fish aquarium, are physical, continuously varying data. This is **analogue data** and needs converting to digital before it can be processed. An **analogue to digital converter (ADC)** is used for this task and these are often built into the input devices themselves.

There is no convenient way to categorise input devices. Consider what is to be collected and whether the data is:

- collected manually by users entering data or selecting from options: keyboard, mouse, tracker ball, touch screens;
- captured automatically (and maybe continuously) without any human intervention: temperature, pressure, light and moisture/humidity sensors;
- an image/sound: scanner, digital camera, video camera, microphones are used in voice activation systems as well as for capturing sound for recording purposes; webcams might provide images to be stored as well as act as a means to video conferencing;
- a response to a control action: joysticks can control physical objects such as remote robotic equipment as well as images on screen; steering wheels can be used in virtual simulators.

This is a continuously expanding list because new ways of getting data into a computer for processing are being developed all the time. With the exception of various sensors, the majority of the above devices rely on physical interaction with the user.

There are other input devices that read data in some way and transmit it directly to the computer system that is going to process the data. These are known as **direct entry devices**.

These would include:

- magnetic stripe readers to read the data on the magnetic stripe on the back of credit cards;
- chip readers, which read data stored in the chip on a bank card;

Revision tip

When describing how data travels through a system it might be necessary to include the transfer of data from the device such as a pressure sensor through an ADC to the processor.

- PIN pads to collect data at Electronic Funds Transfer at Point of Sale (EFTPOS) systems, for example in a supermarket;
- Radio-Frequency Identification (RFID) readers, which wirelessly read data stored in chips on tags attached to goods in stock control systems;
- barcode readers;
- Magnetic Ink Character Readers (MICR), which take pre-printed information from bank cheques;
- Optical Mark Readers (OMR) to read marks on student multiple choice response forms;
- Optical Character Readers (OCR) to read printed or even handwritten text;
- automated number plate recognition systems use high-definition infrared digital cameras to capture an image or a partial image of the number plate and then OCR software to convert the grabbed image(s) to a searchable text string that can be used to search a vehicle registration database.

When collecting data with any of these input devices, it is important to remember that the processing of that data might not be immediate. Some systems require that the data is stored first and then a 'batch' or certain quantity of data is processed together – such as when banks process cheques.

Revision tip

For each of these devices it is necessary to consider its use and relative advantages and disadvantages for any given scenario.

Monitoring and tracking systems

Companies can monitor or log the activities of their employees by a variety of methods. The reasons for carrying out this activity could be to improve productivity, protect corporate resources or to prevent unacceptable behaviour. The methods used could include key-logging, internet monitoring or GPS tracking.

Members of the public can be monitored through the use of surveillance cameras. People who are under surveillance, as a form of punishment, may have to wear an electronic tagging device which uses GPS systems to identify the location of the person.

Call monitoring is the listening and recording of telephone conversations. This is often carried out at call centres. You will often hear a pre-recorded message informing you that your telephone conversation may be recorded for training purposes. The company will use the recordings to help the company improve its customer service, but these recordings could be used as evidence that certain information had been passed between the company and an individual.

When you visit a website that uses cookies for the first time a cookie is downloaded onto your computer. A cookie, or tracking cookie, is a small encrypted text file which is used by the website to tailor or personalise your visit to the site. When you visit the site again you may find that some advertising seems to be targeted to you personally, based on your activity on the website. The website can identify you are a returning visitor because you have their cookie on your computer.

Key-logging uses software to record every keystroke made by a computer user and while a company may use such software for monitoring purposes you need to be aware of the fact that this type of software could be spyware that has been downloaded to your computer. The key-logger records instant messages, email, and any information you type at your keyboard, and then transmits this data to the originator of the software.

Automatic number plate recognition (ANPR) allows a vehicle to be instantly checked against a database of vehicles. This may be used by a police force to identify stolen or uninsured vehicles, or vehicles used to carry out an offence. ANPR is used to help monitor traffic flow on motorways and by speed cameras. You may even have seen AMPR being used at car parks with your car registration number appearing on your car park ticket.

Quick test

Are the following statements true or false?

Input devices can be used to process information.	
Analogue data is a form of binary information.	
Data such as mass (weight) is analogue data.	
A mouse collects data automatically.	
Data on a train ticket can be read by an OCR device.	
A bar code is an input device.	

Output devices

The data processing cycle:

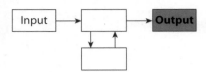

Output devices are used to get data out of a computer system to provide information or instructions for the user or another device. There are many input devices but the number of output devices is fewer. This is because we have a limited number of senses and therefore the number of ways that information can be presented to us as a result of processing is limited. However, it is also important to remember that other devices, such as motors, might be the target for data output.

Computer processors are electronic, digital devices and so the output from the processor is digital data, data that only comprises 0s and 1s (binary data). This data can be used by devices such as computer monitors and printers but some output devices such as a motor or a valve work with analogue data. In these cases the data output by the processor first of all needs converting to an analogue signal by a **digital to analogue converter (DAC)**. An **actuator** is a device which takes a signal from the computer and uses it to operate a device such as a motor or a valve.

There are families of printers and screens:

- Screens/monitors: Cathode Ray Tube (CRT), Thin Film Transistor (TFT), Light Emitting Diode (LED), touch screens
- Printers: laser, inkjet, dot matrix, 3D, wide format

Devices could be grouped by use:

- Presentations: projectors, speakers
- Control devices: motors (used to control robots, cranes and other equipment), buzzers, heaters, lights/lamps

When deciding which output device might be appropriate, the needs of the audience should be considered. For example high-quality, low-quantity printouts might call for an inkjet printer, whereas quick printing of higher volume pages will require a laser printer.

> ### Revision tip
>
> The format of any output needs to be appropriate to the user and the situation, so the advantages and disadvantages of each device need careful consideration.

Quick test

Are the following statements true or false?

Output devices control processes	
Analogue data is produced by the processor	
A 3D printer produces physical output	
An actuator is a type of digital to analogue convertor	
A printer is a suitable output device for a burglar alarm	
Sound is an output device	

Exam-style practice questions

1 Place a tick in the correct column to identify each item as input or output.

	Input	Output
Oxygen level sensor		
TV remote control		
Heater		
Data gloves		
Thermal printer		

[3 marks]

2 What is the purpose of an analogue to digital convertor? [1 mark]

3 State two differences between a laser printer and a dot matrix printer. [2 marks]

4 What input device would be used to input student answers to a multiple choice test? [1 mark]

5 List the input and output devices that are used at the checkout at a supermarket. [3 marks]

6 Why would a set of speakers connected to a computer need a digital to analogue convertor? [1 mark]

7 Iris recognition and fingerprint recognition devices are input devices. Identify a system that each one might be used for. [2 marks]

8 A system is being created for a greenhouse. It will monitor the moisture of the soil in flowerbeds, with sprinklers being activated if the soil becomes too dry. Identify the input and output devices that will be needed. [2 marks]

9 Identify how voice recognition systems can be used in a car and discuss the advantages and disadvantages of having voice recognition systems in cars. [4 marks]

10 A farmer has been considering using Radio Frequency Identification tags for his sheep. What could the tags be used for in this situation? List one advantage and one disadvantage. [3 marks]

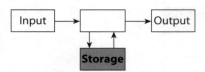
Storage devices and media

The data processing cycle:

Input → [ ] → Output
with **Storage** below

Storage devices are used to keep data for later use, which may be at a further stage in processing (short term) or for archiving purposes (long term).

There are four categories that storage devices can be divided into and these also reflect, generally, the speed at which the devices operate (slow to fast):

- magnetic tape storage used for backup purposes and large-scale data storage;
- optical storage: CD/DVD (for storing music and films), CD/DVD-ROM (to store software such as an interactive encyclopedia), DVD-RAM (provides much faster access to data than a standard DVD), Blu-ray (high capacity: when used for storing movies it offers high definition);
- magnetic disk storage: fixed hard disks (the main storage device in most computers), portable hard disk drives (a portable version of a fixed hard disk);
- solid state memory (uses microchips to store information): pen drives which use USB sockets, flash memory cards (used in mobile phones, digital cameras and gaming devices).

Data on a device can be accessed in one of two ways: direct (or random) access and serial (or sequential) access. With a direct access device data can be located immediately, whereas in a serial access device data has to be read through in sequence until the required data is located. Of the devices listed above, magnetic tape is the only serial access device. Locating a particular item on a direct access device is faster than serial access.

The importance of data backup

Making a **backup** means making an extra copy of stored information that can be used as a replacement in case of a problem such as loss or damage to the original copy.

It can sometimes be difficult to know what to back up. Operating systems and application software can be reinstalled but photographs and videos from a holiday cannot be recreated. Many families choose to back up on CD-ROM for example, or have a removable hard disk drive with copies of important files. Large organisations such as banks or hospitals have to safeguard against file loss or data corruption. They might store information on magnetic tapes which have a very high capacity.

What backup options do users and organisations have?

- A manual unstructured backup involves selecting a number of essential files that need to be copied across onto another disk or flash drive for safe-keeping.

> **Revision tip**
>
> Remember that as well as the standard CD/DVDs which are bought with content preloaded, there are DVD-Rs (can be written to once only) and DVD-RWs (can be rewritten to), which are purchased content free and then written to by the user.

- A full system backup involves copying every single file that is stored on a computer across to another medium. This is often referred to as making an 'image' of the computer. This would be carried out to enable the system to be recreated in case of a complete failure. This copy may be stored off-site.
- Incremental backups are those that are done at regular intervals – sometimes of specific files, such as a stock file – so that a particular point in time can be returned to if necessary.

Reducing file sizes for storage or transmission

Files are often very big, especially picture files. Waiting for a file to download is time-consuming and if a user has to wait for your webpage to download they may well click away from it out of impatience. Your email provider may have a maximum file size that can be attached to an email which is inconvenient.

You could crop an image or reduce the picture resolution to create a smaller file, but for reducing the size of large files, especially for transmission across a network, it is common to compress them. A disadvantage of compressing a picture file is that it changes the amount of detail in the picture, so that after compression the picture can look different to the original

File compression reduces the logical size of a file in order to save disk space and to enable faster transmission over a network or the internet. It results in the creation of a version of the file with the same data but in a size smaller than the original file. A number of files may be compressed together. You may have come across the term 'file zipping' or have used .zip files. File compression can reduce a file's size by 50–90 per cent. The receiver of the files can then restore them to their original format.

Quick test

Are the following statements true or false?

ROM is a type of storage device	
Optical disks are a serial access device	
A copy of a single file is not a backup option	
Any magnetic storage device can be used for backup copies	
Solid state devices are the fastest devices for retrieving information	
All optical storage devices can be rewritten to	

ICT applications – Banking

Visiting the branch of a bank is becoming a thing of the past. Transactions such as checking balances and transferring money, and other services that customers require such as ordering foreign currency and even applying for a loan can be carried out from home.

Telephone banking has been possible for many years. Instead of having to talk to someone at a bank call centre there is now a greater use of voice recognition software, which allows choices from menus to be made and numerical information to be accepted and processed. This may be used in conjunction with keypad data entry.

Internet banking is carried out through the use of secure webpages that provide access to account details and a range of services after secure login has been established.

Many banks are now developing and promoting apps for mobile devices such as smartphones.

You will need to be able to describe phone banking and internet banking, as well as discuss the advantages and disadvantages of internet banking, from the standpoints of both the customer and the bank.

Banking technology and terminology

Electronic Funds Transfer (EFT) is concerned with transferring funds from one bank to another electronically. This can be done with direct data entry devices such as chip and PIN.

Automated teller machines (**ATMs**) are used, among other things, to dispense cash, check balances and top up mobile phone credit. They are found in many public places and have a direct communication link to a bank.

Credit and debit cards are used as an alternative to cash. They can be used to pay for goods and services by means of a chip and PIN reader or by using contactless payment technology.

Cheques are orders to banks to pay someone an amount of money. When processed by the bank they contain information that can be read by an MICR device, which generates an instruction for the transfer of funds. This process may take 4–5 days to complete.

> **Revision tip**
>
> Try to keep up-to-date with emerging technology in this industry. Recent trends are towards contactless payment systems which use RFID systems.

> **Revision tip**
>
> Consider the reasons that people might still want to talk face-to-face with someone in a bank, such as when arranging a mortgage.

Quick test

Are the following statements true or false?

EFT relies on the user having direct contact with both banks involved.	
Cheques are used to transfer money from one person to another.	
Chip and PIN devices are necessary for contactless payment systems to work.	
Telephone banking means that a conversation with a bank employee is needed.	
An ATM lets a customer complete some services without needing to visit a bank.	
Credit cards are an electronic identity card, payment is made with a debit card.	

Exam-style practice questions

1 Place a tick in the correct column to identify each item as magnetic, optical or solid state devices.

	Magnetic	Optical	Solid state
CD/DVD			
Memory stick			
Cassette tape			
Blu-ray			
Removable hard disk drive			

[3 marks]

2 Only one of the below is a serial access device. Put a circle around it.   [1 mark]

CD-ROM   Flash memory card   Fixed hard drive   Pen drive   Magnetic tape

3 Zac has completed the first draft of his course work, which contains many high definition photographs. He has stored it on a CD because of the space needed. You think that Zac has stored it on the wrong type of media. Why? What would be your preferred type of media? Why?   [3 marks]

4 The branch of a multinational bank in your town is closing. What are the advantages to the bank of doing this? What are the disadvantages to the bank's customers of this?   [2, 2 marks]

5 Cloud computing is an alternative way to keep a backup copy of important files. What is this? Describe two advantages and one disadvantage of this arrangement.   [1, 2 marks]

An introduction to computer network hardware

Computer networks enable computers to communicate with each other and share data and information.

In order to understand how networks function it is important to know what hardware devices are involved. Although network configurations vary, only a small number of devices are required to build one. The main components are:

- **Routers**. Connect different computer networks – more commonly used to connect a home computer to the internet.
- **Hubs and switches**. Join together computers and peripheral devices such as printers and storage devices so that they can share files and an internet connection.
- **Bridges.** Allow different networks, between departments in a large organisation for example, to be connected.
- **NIC**s. Network Interface Cards enable a computer to connect with the cable or wireless access points that the network uses.
- **Modems**. Needed to connect to the internet via a telephone line.
- Wireless technology allows devices to connect to a network without physical wires, using radio transmitters and receivers. Two popular systems are Bluetooth and WiFi.

Communicating across a network can be done in two different ways: using cables (twisted pair cable or fibre optic cable), radio waves (wireless). A network in a large organisation is likely to be cabled because this allows greater transmission rates. The home user will likely have a wireless network connecting devices in the home. Fibre optic cables provide faster data transmission than twisted pair (copper) cable.

Evaluating internet-connected devices. 3G and 4G technologies deliver different access capabilities for tablets and smartphones, most notably with speed, but a considerable number of people buy WiFi-only tablets. If your laptop (or desktop) is connected to the internet via a fixed line cable then access is generally faster than with WiFi. Laptops can give you mobile internet access if they are fitted with a SIM card and software, but having mobile connectivity is only as good as the coverage you have. With WiFi-only devices, internet access is restricted by your proximity to a wireless access point.

Computer networks

Setting up a network requires computer hardware, browser software, local wiring infrastructure and an **Internet Service Provider (ISP)** to connect to the internet. The ISP will provide a modem or router that connects the home network to the ISP's servers and internet. Whether the home network is connected via copper wire or fibre optic cable will depend on location. Browser software converts data from the ISP and allows the user to view webpages.

There are three general configurations of network: local area networks (LAN), wireless LAN (WLAN) and wide area networks (WAN).

LANs consist of computers and peripheral devices connected together over a small area such as a school building or office block. Each computer in the

Revision tip

Bluetooth is an example of wireless personal area networking (WPAN). It enables small volume data transfer between devices within a small range (about 10m).

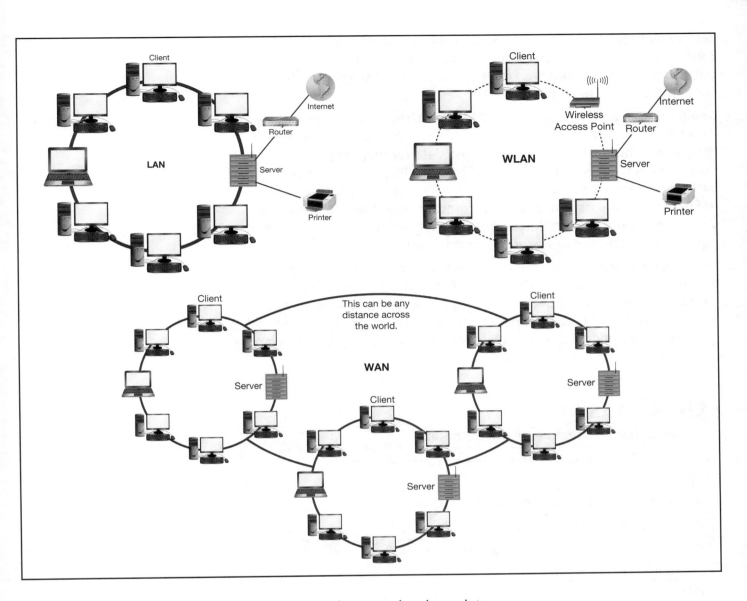

network can be used as a stand-alone computer but can also share data and software over the network. Each computer on the LAN is known as a client and the clients are usually connected to the network server by cable.

WLANs are different from LANs because they use a wireless link (of radio transmitters and receivers) to connect computers together instead of using cables. To make the wireless connection possible, wireless access points are required, meaning that a computer on the network needs Bluetooth and/or WiFi capability. Routers will also allow several computers to access the internet through the wireless access point at the same time.

WANs connect LANs to each other over a wide geographical area by using routers or a broadband modem. The internet itself is a WAN. WANs can transmit data across the network in a number of ways: high-speed telephone lines, microwave links, fibre optic cables or satellite links. WANs are more likely to be used by large organisations that have branches in many countries and may use all of these methods of transmitting data.

Satellite systems

There are a number of different satellite systems currently in use. You will be familiar with global positioning systems GPS, what the majority of us know as SatNav. This system allows anyone with a GPS receiver to

> **Revision tip**
>
> There are two types of LAN: client-server and peer-to-peer. Be sure that you know the difference between them.

determine their exact location. There are 24 satellites surrounding the Earth which are continuously transmitting their location. The GPS receiver calculates its position based on the triangulation of information from a minimum of three satellite signals.

Geographic Information Systems (GIS) capture, store, check and display data related to positions on the Earth's surface. They connect data with geography. This does not just mean using data for mapping exercises. Environmental agencies (and insurers) can use GIS to predict flood patterns, an energy company wanting to erect electricity pylons can use GIS to find the path that disrupts forest areas as little as possible, a delivery company can use GIS to help with delivery drive-times as well as using data to help site new stores or distribution centres.

Media communication systems are those that allow communication and data exchange among a large number of individuals across long distances via, for example, email, teleconferencing and internet forums. All these enable a number of users to interact with each other. On the other hand, traditional mass media channels such as TV, radio and magazines, promote one-to-many communication.

Quick test

Are the following statements true or false?

Data transmission with copper cable is faster than fibre optic cable.	
A LAN does not require wireless access points.	
A WAN is a network of networks.	
One advantage of a WLAN is that users can be anywhere in a building.	
ISPs need to provide special browser software with the modem.	
A hub is only needed when the internet is being used.	

ICT applications 1

The internet and intranets

The **internet** is an international WAN, a network of networks, that allows users to use email, exchange files, browse the world wide web or to chat using text or voice.

The world wide web is a part of the internet. A web browser allows the user to access information stored on the internet through websites. Websites are collections of pages of information that are linked together by **hyperlinks**. Clicking on a hyperlink will take the user to other pages within a particular website or to another website altogether.

Each webpage has a unique address, a uniform resource locator (URL), which describes the path to a particular file or resource stored on a remote server.

For example:

http://www.bbc.co.uk/news/technology-36596070

Protocol	Hostname	Domain name			File path	Filename
		Second level domain	Sub domain	Top level domain		
http://	www	.bbc	.co	.uk/	news/	technology-3659670

Users access the internet through an Internet Service Provider (ISP) using an allocated username and password. In many countries the ISP is required to keep a log of the internet activity of its subscribers.

With networks having many users, all requiring access to the same internet connection, a **proxy server** is needed. This acts as a gateway between users and the internet.

Organisations often choose to restrict access to the internet but need a way of sharing and using resources in a manner which gives the same feel as using the internet. This is done by creating an **intranet**, a network offering internal restricted access. Users can access web-based material, share files and communicate via email but all the data transfer takes place within the local network.

Revision tip

Contrast the advantages and disadvantages of internet and intranet use.

Effective use of the internet

The internet provides access to a gigantic 'library' of information from the millions of websites around the world. While access to all this information is a reason for connecting to it, it is only one aspect of this world-wide telecommunications network. Among other things, users can send and receive email, share photos and video clips, carry out online shopping and banking, make video-calls. The speed at which access to this information is achieved is another reason that the internet is so popular, and as applications get more sophisticated so does the physical infrastructure that delivers the data.

School management systems

Within a school setting, administration, teachers and students all need access to various collections of information. Teachers and students require access to a teaching and learning network with a shared area, where resources can be exchanged, and private areas to work on their own materials. School management also need a separate area for purposes such as: financial, human resources, timetabling, examination, assessment and reporting.

Teachers can access class registers to record attendance at the beginning of each day, as well as attendance at each lesson. The school timetable will be created using one module which then allows for the creation of timetables for all teachers and students. You should be able to describe how a school management system can be used to organise, for example, examination timetables and teaching cover/substitution.

This vast collection of data will be stored on servers that all users will be accessing so it is vitally important that each area is protected, with permissions for access applied carefully and precisely. In some settings the school may have separate LANs, one for teaching and learning and another for management. These would be connected by a router so that management has access to teaching and learning resources.

Booking systems

Booking systems such as those used by theatres, cinemas and airlines rely on files being updated immediately. This is important to avoid double booking of appointments, seats and tickets. Booking systems such as these which use online processing are likely to use a WAN.

For example, after logging into an airline's system a ticket could be booked by:

- choosing departure and destination airports;
- selecting dates/times;
- selecting seats and additional options such as meals and extra baggage;
- entering personal details;
- selecting method and making payment;
- printing e-tickets to use as a boarding pass for the flight.

> **Revision tip**

Consider the advantages and disadvantages of online booking systems.

Quick test

Are the following statements true or false?

The internet is a collection of linked LANs.	
A proxy server is a secure copy of a company's data server.	
An intranet is internal to a company or organisation.	
School management systems allow free access by users to stored data.	
A pupil registration system is a type of booking system.	
Hyperlinks provide a clickable connection between webpages.	

ICT applications 2

Chapter 4
Computer
networks and
the effects of
using them

Medicine

Within clinics and hospitals, computer systems and technology are used extensively in both administration and patient care. Patient records are available to doctors, which are reviewed and updated after consultations. Doctors can issue prescriptions from their workstations, which are received and dispensed at the pharmacy. The clinic will operate a LAN system but that network will probably have a connection to the local hospital network so that patients can be referred to specialists. Within a hospital the administration systems hold enormous amounts of organisational data as well as patient data. Treatment can also be monitored by technology, such as the sensors that measure a variety of physical processes like heart rate, blood pressure, respiration and temperature.

Expert systems

Expert systems are created by collecting knowledge from experts to form a knowledge base. Built around this is an inference engine and a rules base which attempt to mimic human reasoning from given information to solve a problem. A special interface allows users to input and output data/information. Expert systems should reduce the time taken to solve problems while at the same time requiring a less skilled workforce. Answers will always be consistent but any error in the knowledge or rules base will mean incorrect decisions are made. A medical diagnosis system would be useful to help identify and treat tropical disease. Other example uses of expert systems are helping mechanics to locating faults in a car engine, or in assessing the data from geological surveys when undertaking mining exploration.

Revision tip

Consider other applications where expert systems could be used.

Libraries

The computer network in a library will have one file server holding data on the books and other media that the library lends to borrowers, and another which holds details of library members. This network will also be connected to other library networks so that requests for books from other libraries can be made. The ISBN number on a book and on a member's library card can be read by a barcode reader but increasingly books, CDs, DVDs, jigsaws and other items are tracked using Radio-Frequency Identification (RFID) technology. Thumb or fingerprinting technology may also be used to identify a borrower. As well as updating the details on the book/media file the system will also, at regular intervals (often daily), run an application process to identify books that are or are about to go overdue so that reminder letters/emails can be sent to the borrower concerned.

Modelling

A model is a mathematical representation of a real system, created to help predict what might happen when input variables are changed. In a financial model this might consider how changes in various income streams will affect a company's profitability, and in a traffic management model the effects of introducing roadworks or traffic lights at a road junction could be analysed. Models are important because various scenarios can be tried out in advance or where a real life 'trial' would not be possible, such as the government investigating whether to raise a tax level or a company exploring the effects of a product price increase. However, it is important to remember that, like expert systems, the results that they produce are dependent on the accuracy of the data/formulae that they are built around.

On a smaller scale, spreadsheets are often used to create personal financial models. This allows you to create a household budget and to then make changes to the variables, which can help you to assess the impact on the data of decisions that you make.

Quick test

Are the following statements true or false?

Computer systems can help diagnose a patient's disease.	
Librarians rely on detailed information stored on index cards.	
A computer chess game is an example of an expert system.	
A flight simulator is an example of a computer model.	
To ensure data security, patient records are stored on stand-alone computers.	
A library information system is an expert system.	

Business and personal communication

There are many ways that ICT enables people to communicate, either within organisations and for business purposes, or for personal communication.

Email addresses are allocated to people within organisations: an.employee@mycompany.com or a.student@myschool.sch.uk. Outside work or school most people have email with a free email service such as anybody99@gmail.com or anybody101@hotmail.co.uk.

Accessing email messages requires an email application program to be open so that messages can be opened and read. Instant messaging (IM), a system which enables messages to be sent and received immediately (real-time communication), is often built into, but not dependent on, social networking applications.

It is sometimes difficult to know how someone has reacted to an IM or an email. **Video conferencing** is more personal and allows many users to join a discussion and be able to see each other's reactions. An enhancement of this is web conferencing, where participants can also share electronic content: documents, images, video stream.

Voice Over Internet Protocol (**VOIP**) – using the internet to make telephone calls – is increasingly popular, enabling audio conferencing to take place, which is video conferencing without the visual element.

Electronic faxing is replacing traditional physical faxing because an internet-connected computer, scanner and printer can replace the facsimile machine.

Weblogs (blogs) are online personal or business journals, used to present ideas, articles and links to other websites. Some interactivity is possible, with readers of the blog being able to post comments and provide feedback. Tweets are sometimes referred to as micro-blogs. Twitter is a communication application allowing members to connect by following ideas or topics (identified by a hash tag, for example, #igcse), not just people (identified by, for example, @joebloggs).

Forums are interactive websites that allow users to take part in discussions. Sometimes a forum is concerned with a particular topic only, but often will have a number of active threads, or conversations, going on at any one time. Users post their comments to the website. A moderated forum has an administrator, or moderator, who checks the user's post before publishing it to the forum. The reason for this is that the moderator is checking that no offensive, racist or hateful content is being submitted, or even sometimes that the post is relevant to the nature of the forum. An unmoderated forum has no such checking mechanism and this can mean that offensive and inappropriate material is posted. Another risk of unmoderated forums is users posting messages for spamming and phishing purposes. Moderated forums offer a certain level of security because the moderator functions as a filter, blocking attempts to use posts inappropriately. Users who frequently try to break the rules applied by the moderator risk being banned from the forum.

> **Revision tip**
>
> Know what hardware is necessary to set up a video conference.

Wikis are collaborative websites that are built and grown by users adding to an online database. The popularity and usefulness of the site depends on the accuracy and reliability of the information presented.

Social networking sites such as Facebook, QZone and VK allow people to communicate with each other and create friendship groups in a very interactive online environment. With their billions of users, social networking sites are also popular with businesses for advertising products.

In any organisation it is important that users only have access to the areas and data that they are supposed to have. Setting and managing access rights is the responsibility of a network administrator.

User IDs (usernames) and **passwords** are essential when logging into a workstation. The network system software will check that the ID is valid on the network and that the given password is connected to the ID. If the details are good the system will make available the hardware and software resources that the user's access rights allow. Sometimes systems require additional identifying details: a unique answer to a question, a security code on a wristband, an electronic code generator, a fingerprint or an iris scan. These are all authentication techniques.

In many organisations data is **encrypted** to protect it further, so that if data is accessed by an unauthorised user it cannot be read or understood.

Revision tip

Employers may investigate a job applicant's social networking profile in order to gain additional background information prior to interview.

Revision tip

Passwords can be described as strong or weak. Strong passwords are hard to guess and will usually be more than eight characters long, contain a mixture of lowercase and uppercase letters, numbers, and even some allowable punctuation characters. Weak passwords are those such as the word 'password', '12345678', your mum's name, your pet's name. Strong passwords are much less likely to be guessed.

Revision tip

Ensure that the elements of the Data Protection Act are known and understood.

Quick test

Are the following statements true or false?

aname#ictgcse.org is a valid email address.	
IM does not require special application software.	
Twitter is a social networking site.	
Weak passwords are easily guessed.	
A passport number would not be a good authentication detail.	
VOIP allows visual contact to be made between callers.	

Locating information on the internet can be done directly by typing the URL of the resource (webpage or file) into your browser. Often you will be using the internet to search for information, and so instead of typing in a URL you will need to use a search engine.

There are many search engines available. Whether you are a user of Google, Ask, Dogpile or DuckDuckGo, they all perform a similar task – searching for content based on words you enter. Although different search engines may work slightly differently from each other, key words are essential for any basic search. A simple search will quickly produce information and images – not all of which may be relevant.

Advanced searches allow more specific information to be provided, even asking that some keywords are ignored. For example, when searching for information about a computer mouse:

Google

Advanced Search

Find pages with...

all these words:	mouse
this exact word or phrase:	computer
any of these words:	input or device
none of these words:	mammal animal
numbers ranging from:	to

Then narrow your results by...

language:	English ▼

If you cannot find an advanced search dialogue box like the Google example you can always use the advanced features manually, as in this example from DuckDuckGo:

 mouse input OR or OR device "computer" -mammal -animal 🔍

Revision tip

In an advanced search, quotation marks indicate that the term must be included, a minus sign indicates that the term must not appear in the results. Boolean operators are also options, suggesting that either of the different terms can be included (OR), that certain combinations must be included (AND) or they should not be included (NOT).

For even the simplest search you will be faced with tens of thousands of results. A number of the links at the top of the results list will also be sponsored pages (the providers are paying to have their link at the top). Most people will not bother to look beyond the first couple of pages of results. There is a danger of being overwhelmed with choices, especially as at the bottom of the search page there may be a list of alternative or related search queries to click on. You need to be quite disciplined when carrying out searches. Go back and refine your search criteria. This can mean that searching for relevant information takes quite a time.

You need to remember that the results that are returned by the search engine might not be relevant. This could be because your search criteria were not specific enough. Anyone can write something and post it on the internet. With clever indexing and optimisation their page may appear high in the returned results, but that does not make it reliable or accurate. It is important that you make your search criteria as precise as possible and then get into the habit of carefully evaluating the information in the returned pages that you choose to read. Read the content of three or four promising pages, comparing the content for reliability and accuracy. For example, you might ask yourself if the information is fact, opinion or propaganda? Does it display bias? Does the information seem to be valid and well-researched? Is there any supporting evidence? Is it up-to-date?

Emailing has already been briefly mentioned. Apart from sending a message to an individual friend or colleague, it is possible to send messages to lists or groups of people and to have the email addresses of some of those recipients hidden. When sending to a number of people, the email addresses of those people could all appear in the 'To' option. Often you may be sending the message specifically to one person but out of courtesy want to send it to others as well. In this case use the 'Cc' (carbon copy) option. All those who receive the message will see that the other people have also received the same message. Sometimes it is better that the recipient email addresses are not visible to everyone who receives the email, for personal and data protection reasons. Such an example might be a holiday company mailing list. In this case the Bcc (blind carbon copy) would be used, with the 'To' option addressed to either the sender or an unmonitored email address.

For example, this email has been sent from the secretary at All Computers Inc. to a list of recipients who form a distribution list or contact group called 'All Sales Reps Europe'. Each person on the list will receive the email but will not see the email addresses of the other recipients. The secretary will also receive the email. Some email applications may list each email address separately rather than group by the list's name.

When using email you need to be aware of issues surrounding your use of it. The country that you are emailing from (or even into) may have strong filtering/censorship policies in place, so it is vital that you avoid contentious or inflammatory vocabulary. It is also general netiquette that you are polite and respect other people's views, keeping your language appropriate to the reader of the email, remembering to never WRITE EVERYTHING IN CAPTIALS, as it gives the impression that you are angry. If you are emailing within a LAN such as a school or small business there may be rules about the language and style of writing you can use. Some organisations will have an encryption policy that applies to certain emails, for example if financial information is being emailed to someone outside of the organisation, or an attachment to an email might have password protection.

From:	Secretary@AllComputersInc.com;
To:	Secretary@AllComputersInc.com;
Cc:	
Bcc:	All Sales Reps Europe;
Subject:	July 2016 Newsletter

All Sales Reps Europe
Distribution list

Khalel Khan
KKhan@allcomputersinc.com
External contact

Paul Smith
PSmith@allcomputersinc.com
External contact

Petra Svenland
PSvenland@allcomputesinc.com
External contact

Philip Jones
PJones@allcomputersinc.com
External contact

Ullrich Mirtzof
UMirtzof@allcomputersinc.com
External contact

> ### Revision tip
>
> It is important that the multiple ways of sending a message to a variety of individuals and groups is fully understood.

Quick test

Are the following statements true or false?

Cc-ing an email ensures that anonymity is maintained.	
Distribution lists cannot be used in the 'To' option of an email message.	
Use Bcc so that email recipients do not know who else is a recipient.	
Web browsers all perform the same task but in slightly different ways.	
Advanced searches will return 100 per cent relevant results.	
Using 'Mouse' AND 'Wireless' in a search engine returns suggestions where both terms are included	

Exam-style practice questions

1 Place a tick in the correct column to identify whether the device is needed in a network. [3 marks]

	Needed	Not-needed
Bridge		
Bluetooth		
Switch		
Modem		
RFID tags		

2 Place a tick in the correct column to identify whether each statement is true or false. [2 marks]

	True	False
A LAN connects computers over a small area		
A WLAN does not allow connection to the internet		
A WAN must have cable connections		
LAN users cannot share an internet connection		
WANs enable very fast data transfer between multinational organisations		

3 Place a tick in the correct column to identify whether each statement is true or false. [2 marks]

	True	False
An expert system has an Information Engine		
A booking system has to work in real time		
A school management system needs all data areas to be fully shared		
The LAN in a doctor's surgery will probably be connected to a local hospital network		
Weather forecasters use modelling systems		

4 Outline one advantage and one disadvantage of using a LAN compared to stand-alone computers. [2 marks]

5 Identify two hardware devices that would convert a LAN into a WLAN. [2 marks]

6 Using HyperText Transfer Protocol (HTTP) a user can access the World Wide Web. FTP is another internet protocol. What is this used for? [1 mark]

7 A mechanic uses an expert system to diagnose faults with a car engine. Describe how the expert system does this. [3 marks]

8. A manufacturing company's factory covers a large area in a town. It has been decided that a network will be created to allow information to be accessible across the site. The company management team are choosing between a LAN and a WLAN. Describe one advantage and one disadvantage to the company of choosing a WLAN rather than a standard LAN. [2 marks]

9. A civil engineer is using a modelling system to test the design for a new motorway bridge. Describe two benefits of using the modelling system. [2 marks]

10. A bakery uses a LAN in its administration and shares information via the company intranet. The owners of the bakery want to establish a website with an online ordering system. The ICT company the bakery uses have said that this is not possible with their current network arrangement. Explain why the ICT company have said this. [1 mark]

    What change must be made to allow the online ordering system to work? [1 mark]

    State one advantage and one disadvantage of the bakery's system carrying out the changes. [2 marks]

11. Social networking sites such as Facebook allow members to communicate by instant messaging. Why is this better than the member profiles providing email addresses to put people in touch? [2 marks]

12. A large multinational pharmaceutical company has research facilities all over Europe. The research facilities need to share information with each other. One company director says that they need to set up a website so that they can share information. Is the director correct? Why/why not? [2 marks]

IT and employment

Newspaper headlines remind us of the number of people who lose their jobs because of computers, but this is only half the story. Jobs are lost, but jobs can also be changed for the better and new jobs created because of the use of computers.

Technology has different impacts depending on where it is introduced. In manufacturing, dirty and dangerous jobs have been replaced by machinery. In commercial situations the emergence of word processing has led to the disappearance of the role of the typist. Shops have always needed people to serve and deal with customers but the growth of online shopping and self-service tills is changing this.

The emerging issues that the introduction of ICT creates are:

- retraining – due to the changing nature of an employee's work;
- deskilling – lower levels of skill needed;
- better working environment – robots have taken over dirty or dangerous jobs;
- reduced costs – fewer employees needed;
- higher productivity – automated processes can run for 24 hours a day;
- consistency – computer-controlled systems produce identical products.

The last three bullet points above are advantages of making use of computer controlled systems – as seen by the company owner. You need to be able to discuss the effects of introducing these systems, remembering that the company owner and the company workforce may have different views.

There is also an increasing number of people who, because of the internet, have been able to start small businesses, which they run from home through their own website. Jobs in and with technology are expanding: programming and system design/maintenance, website design, smartphone app creation, network managers, social media managers, and so on.

Working patterns

Emerging technology is allowing employers to become more accommodating to employees' working patterns. Flexible hours working allows an employee to work their required hours at times more suitable to them, with maybe the only requirement to be in the office between certain hours. Since technology allows work to take place at locations other than an office desk, flexible working can allow employees to work at home or off-site for part of the week. This is a little different to **teleworking**, where people work entirely at home using the internet to communicate and share files. Some organisations might allow employees to work all their hours in fewer days (compressed work weeks) or give days off in lieu instead of paying overtime (time banks).

For many people their work (career, ambition)/lifestyle (health, leisure, family) balance is important and there is a growing realisation that there needs to be a shift away from salaries and status to a more flexible working environment. Employers are recognising that they need to meet

Revision tip

Think about the advantages and disadvantages of introducing IT into the workplace.

Revision tip

Be able to describe the advantages and disadvantages of job-sharing.

the demands of employees if they are to retain or recruit the best for their organisation.

The emergence of internet-enabled laptop/tablet computers, WiFi technology and the use of cloud storage, coupled with an ever-increasing internet availability, is driving this change to working patterns. Workers can work on projects without physically being in the same location. Files can be transferred securely via the internet; smartphones and instant messaging keep the team connected; sharing data in cloud storage allows data to be shared by a range of devices, by anyone, anywhere and a variety of application software keeps all devices synchronised.

Quick test

Are the following statements true or false?

The changing nature of certain jobs could involve retraining.	
Working entirely at home is an example of flexible place working.	
Compressed work weeks involves fitting as many hours as possible into a week.	
Before cloud storage, employees could not have worked from home.	
Employers are becoming more responsive to employees' needs.	
An employee might be able to work wherever internet access is available.	

Health issues

How computers are used and how equipment is arranged can lead to significant health problems for computer users. Problems can develop in the neck, back, elbows and wrists because of bad posture. Staring at computer screens can have an effect on eyesight and cause headaches. **Repetitive strain injury** (RSI) is caused by repeating an action over and over again without rest. Laser printers give off ozone, which can cause breathing difficulties. There are strategies and devices that can minimise these problems, such as: where on the desk is your mouse? Are wrists/forearms supported? Do you have an anti-glare screen? Is your laser printer a safe distance away from you? Could you benefit from an ergonomically designed keyboard?

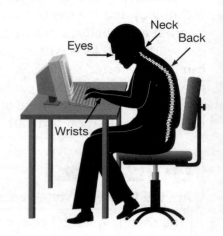

Physical safety in an ICT-based environment

In addition to health issues, the risk of physical danger also needs consideration. Exposed wires present a risk of possible electrocution, and overloaded sockets could cause a fire. If equipment is not well ventilated, fires can result from overheated components. Trailing cables between desks or over the floor are a trip hazard. For each of these potential danger points there are sensible strategies for prevention: do not allow food and drink near computers; ensure that plugs are wired properly; do not overload power sockets; ensure equipment and rooms are properly ventilated; use cable ducts or tape to keep wires safely together; where possible use wireless connections.

> ## Revision tip
>
> Be aware of potential hazards regarding health and physical safety, but also know the solutions to these problems.

Commercial and ethical considerations

Online shopping is on the increase. Many commercial businesses with a physical shop have an online presence and there are many shops that operate entirely online. Having an online presence has tremendous advantages for both the business itself (wider customer base, no need to be located in a populated/expensive area) and the customer (wider choice, comparisons between products, can be done at any hour, anywhere) and yet there are still many people who choose not to shop online. People often like to see the products or be able to try them on, or simply enjoy the experience of browsing the racks and shelves of shops.

Electronic Point Of Sale (EPOS) and **Electronic Funds Transfer Point Of Sale** (EFTPOS) are used by the vast majority of shops to track purchases, enabling stock control, reordering and payment systems to collect data about activity from the checkout. Customers can pay for purchases by chip and PIN readers as well as contactless payment systems.

There are many moral and ethical dimensions to consider when access to ICT is raised. For each consideration in the following list there are both advantages and disadvantages:

* people can share information and conduct business 24 hours a day;
* small businesses can be run via the internet from home, not the high street;
* improved robotics means that products can be made more quickly, precisely and cheaply.

Creating an ICT solution presents legal, moral and ethical considerations. What may be culturally acceptable or legal in one country might not be in another. Religious commentary in countries differs greatly. Online solutions are often accessible outside the country they were written for/developed in, but might be blocked by other countries based on their own moral, ethical or legal standards. Whether a solution is 'right' or 'wrong' depends on many factors, and you need to be prepared to consider the impact of a suggested use of ICT.

There is no international organisation that controls the way in which the internet operates. Should the internet be policed? For example, perhaps this would prevent illegal material being available. But would all participating countries agree on a decision given the cultural, political and religious differences involved? Who would pay for it?

Quick test

Are the following statements true or false?

Spending many hours texting could result in RSI.	
Having drinks on a computer desk poses a safety risk.	
Customers will always want to try on clothes in a shop.	
Contactless payments are possible via an online shop.	
Policing the internet should be the responsibility of one country.	
Commercial businesses can operate without a physical shop.	

The need for copyright

Copyright means that the owners of the material, for example software, music, films and books, have the right to keep, sell, distribute or give away copies of that material as they wish. Some materials are free of copyright meaning that the owners or developers of that resource agree that it can be freely distributed. If material is copied or downloaded without permission the person making the copy is, in most countries, breaking the law.

Software is available on CD, DVD or can be downloaded, and is usually protected by copyright. Copyright law means that something cannot be copied and given away, or rented out without permission. It cannot be used on a network unless a licence has been bought. It is important to check that any installed software is genuine by looking for a product key or a security label. Copyrighted, genuine software will also be guaranteed virus free.

Copyright protection and trying to prevent the 'pirating' of software is a major concern for developers, big or small. Sometimes activation codes are required, which are sent to you by email as part of the installation process. Manufacturers produce special packaging labels or even CD/DVD disks with holograms to enable users to see whether the material is genuine. It is possible that software will not run unless another device is active, such as critical files that are held on a separate CD.

Open source software is offered by the developer with source code that anyone can inspect or modify. Some open source software, such as Open Office which your school may use, may be downloaded for free.

Revision tip

Be aware of the features of the UK Copyright, Designs and Patents Act (amended 2014).

Microprocessor-controlled devices in the home

ICT has not only had an impact on our workplaces, it is also having an enormous impact in our homes. This is not simply about the home use of the internet; many of our household devices have a microprocessor and the development of 'smart' household goods is growing. A microprocessor in a device allows it to be programmed to function in different ways.

The introduction of microprocessor devices into the home has positive as well as negative aspects which you will need to give careful consideration. The introduction of labour-saving devices such as washing machines and dishwashers has had a positive effect on our lifestyles as many things do not need doing manually. They can give people more leisure time and frequent opportunity to leave the home, but this does not always lead to better social interaction or more exercise. In addition, people can become preoccupied with continuously upgrading expensive devices.

Microprocessors are used to control applications in the home such as a central heating system or burglar alarm. When describing how these devices work it is important to consider the processing that is necessary and then identify how the system collects data for input and how the output data is going to be used. For example, in a central heating system analogue data from temperature sensors is collected and will need converting to digital for processing. The temperature is compared with a required temperature and output will be a signal to turn a heater on or off. This signal must be converted back to analogue to control the actuator (see 'Input and output devices' for more on these devices and data conversion).

The analogue data of temperature, humidity or moisture which could be monitored in order to control the heaters and sprinklers of a glasshouse would need similar processing.

Turtle-graphics allow a user to program a series of commands controlling the movement of a cursor on screen or a floor-based robot.

> **Revision tip**
>
> Think of other computer-controlled systems such as traffic lights and pedestrian crossings, and identify the input data/devices, the processing required, the output data/devices that are involved.

Quick test

Are the following statements true or false?

Microprocessors can be used to control household appliances.	
A refrigerator is not a computer-controlled appliance.	
Copyright law only identifies the resource creator.	
It is illegal to copy and distribute software without the creator's permission.	
Open source software can be downloaded without payment.	
Computer-controlled devices need no input.	

Exam-style practice questions

1 A supermarket has installed new self-service checkout technology with EFTPOS capability. Tick three advantages to the supermarket of using this technology. [3 marks]

	✓
Better monitoring of stock levels	
Fewer damaged goods reported	
Higher levels of stock maintained	
Less cash handled at the checkout	
No customer queue build-up	
Customers will spend more	
Fewer staff required at checkouts	

2 Place a tick in the correct column to identify whether each statement is true or false. [3 marks]

	True	False
Copyright law exists to protect the income of resource creators		
A washing machine is a microprocessor-controlled device		
An alarm clock is not a microprocessor-controlled device		
Job-sharing is an example of flexible hours working		
Contactless payments can be made at EFTPOS terminals		

3 Identify three appliances in a family kitchen that are microprocessor-controlled. [3 marks]

4 Identify two potential physical safety hazards that computer users need to be aware of. For each hazard suggest a measure that can be taken to avoid it. [2 marks]

5 Software developers and publishers work hard to prevent software piracy. State one physical and one electronic method that they might use to do this. [2 marks]

6 Wireless networks (WLANs) enable employees to work in locations other than at an office desk. Give two example tasks that a WLAN allows. [2 marks]

7 Outline the difference between retraining and deskilling. [2 marks]

8 An aquarium for tropical fish has its temperature and oxygen levels controlled by a computer system. Describe the inputs, processing and outputs that the system generates and identify the devices needed to achieve this. [6 marks]

9 'A controlled internet would help to protect vulnerable groups and young people by restricting access and content.' Do you agree with this statement? Outline why you do/do not.   [3 marks]

10 A library has all the information about its books, CDs, DVDs and other media stored in a database. These details used to be stored on a huge collection of index cards. Outline two advantages to borrowers and researchers of this change.   [2 marks]

11 A distribution company uses robots in its warehouses to collect products from shelves and return them to a human operator who packs them for shipping to customers. Discuss the advantages and disadvantages of using robots for the company.   [3 marks]

Describe two ways in which work for employees will change.   [2 marks]

File structure and terminology

Collections of data are all around us and we want to be able to search and analyse this data easily. The collection, or file, of data needs structure in order for it to be manipulated.

A file is a collection of related, structured data. Any situation where data is gathered and saved gives rise to a data file, which will need structuring in order to make it useful. An address or contact list, the results of a survey being carried out, membership details for clubs and societies, the content of school reports: all of these are collections of data that we expect to be in some sort of order and have some kind of structure.

For example, a library has a **file** containing all the data about every book it has. The details about each book form a **record** and within the record each piece of data about the book, such as title or author name, is called a **field**. Each record has the same set of fields, which provides structure – the **record structure**.

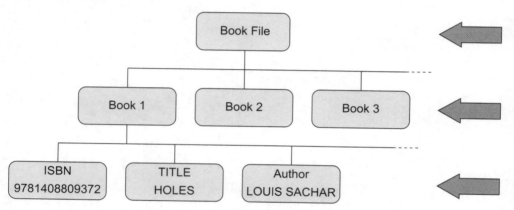

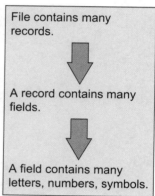

File contains many records.

A record contains many fields.

A field contains many letters, numbers, symbols.

In order to sort or search the records in a file there needs to be a unique identifier. In the book file the field ISBN is unique. Other data items such as passport numbers, telephone numbers and car licence plates are all unique identifiers. These special fields are called key fields or record keys. Sometimes there is no unique data item in a record that can act as a record key and so one will be created.

Care should be taken when choosing file names. Some software may struggle with overly long names. It is not a good idea to use punctuation and some software will also object to the use of spaces. Keep them meaningful and short. In your filing system, 'Analogue_v_digital_data' will be better than 'Last weeks homework for Mr Stobart'. The same ideas apply to choosing field names: FirstName and FamilyName are better than Name1 and Name2.

Files can be flat or relational. A **flat file database** is one that only has a single table of data. A **relational database** has data held in a number of tables where links, called relationships, are created to connect the tables together. A relational database allows data to be searched much more effectively and efficiently than a flat file database.

In a relational database the tables are linked by record keys. One record will have two keys, its own (**primary key**) and one pointing to a record in another table (**foreign key**).

> ### Revision tip
>
> Data is stored in rows (records) and columns (fields) in a two-dimensional table. Partly for this reason data is referred to as being stored in a table.

Here is the record structure from a car salesman's relational database which has two related tables.

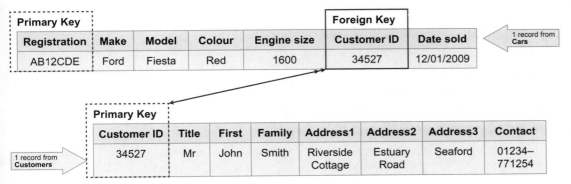

Relationship types connected to the database section of the syllabus are:

- one-to-one, where the foreign key in one record can only ever match one other primary key in another table. This does not occur very often – one customer can only ever have bought one car – and for these to work there must be an identical number of records in each table;
- one-to-many, where for one primary key in a record there are many matches to other foreign keys in another table, as in the diagram above – one customer may have bought more than one car.

Data-handling situation

A library has quite complex data-processing needs. A simple relational database could contain 3 tables:

- books: the book's ISBN is the primary key;
- members: a membership ID is created as a primary key;
- borrowed: a table containing a record for each book currently with borrowers (records added when borrowed and deleted when returned).

Primary Key

ISBN	Title	Author	Classification	Hard/Soft cover	Pages	Available
978034087046	Beginner's Russian	Rachel Farmer	Languages	Soft	246	N

Primary Key / **Foreign Key**

Member ID	First	Family	Address	Contact	ISBN1	ISBN2	ISBN3
AB1234	Colin	Stobart	Estuary Cottage	01234-123456	978034087046		

Primary Key / **Foreign Key**

ISBN	Member ID	Date Return
978034087046	AB1234	30/08/2014

Although it would seem that the Book → Members relationship should be one-to-one, the number of books is not identical to the number of members, so the relationship type is described as one-to-many. The same is true of Book → Borrowed.

> **Revision tip**
>
> Consider the processing that would take place between these tables for a book to be borrowed and then returned.

Quick test

Are the following statements true or false?

A relational database consists of one large multi-dimensional table.	
A foreign key can be duplicated.	
A relational database allows complex searching to take place.	
A record in a relational database need not have a primary key.	
A suitable primary key in a patient database would be the patient name.	
In a flat file database there is only one data table.	

The operations that a database can carry out on an item of data depend on its type, as does the way in which the data is actually stored. So, before a database is created it is vital to consider the fields in the record structure and determine their data type.

What data type	When to use it
Text/Alphanumeric	Text. There may be a limit to how long the data is – often 255 characters.
Number	Any number type. Specifying the number of decimal places is possible. A number with no decimal places is an integer, one with decimal places is a real number.
Date/Time	Formats can vary: dd/mm/yyyy, mm/dd/yyyy for example.
Currency	For example: £, $, €.
Boolean/Logical	Only two alternatives, for example: yes/no, true/false, on/off.
OLE (Object Linked and Embedded)	A graph, video clip, picture, sound file.

It is important that fields have the correct data type assigned to them because this will affect the operations that can be done with them. For example, dates and currency could be assigned as a text field which would allow the data to be displayed correctly but you would not be able to make logical comparisons or perform calculations with them.

Revision tip

A knowledge of OLE is required but not of how to implement it.

In the library database there might be these fields and types:

Field name	Example data	Data type	Comment
Title	Holes	Text	
Cost	£12.99	Currency	Set to £ with 2 decimal places
Available	Y	Boolean	Can only be Y or N

Sorting, searching and querying

Sorting a data set rearranges it, putting it into a different order. The result is the whole data set and not just a part of it. Sometimes a requirement is for more than one sorting order to be applied at the same time, for example sorting a set of students by Surname within Gender.

Searching a data set results in only the selection of records, a subset that fulfil the search criteria, the conditions used to define the search. Searches can be made using the comparison operators < (less than), > (greater than), ≤ (less than or equal to) and ≥ (greater than or equal to), and the logical conditions AND, OR, NOT, LIKE. Additionally, wildcards can be used to search through text fields. An asterisk (*) represents one or more characters in a text string, while a question mark (?) represents a single character.

Examples:

DateOfBirth > 2000	Returns records where the DateOfBirth is later than the year 2000.
Available = "Y" AND Category = "Biography"	Returns records of books of available biographies.
Author Like "Wh?te"	Returns records with White or Whyte as Authors.
Model Like "*ship"	Returns records of all transport such as *battle*ship, *air*ship, *steam*ship and so on.

Quick test

Are the following statements true or false?

A search will always return a subset of the dataset.	
An amount of money could be assigned a data type of number if no currency symbol is needed.	
The results of a cricket match (win, draw, tie, lose) could be assigned a data type of Boolean.	
OrderDate Like ??/10/2016 returns any order made in October 2016.	
It is only possible to apply one sort criterion to a dataset.	
In a school database, student identification photographs will have a data type of OLE.	

Exam-style practice questions

1 A dance teacher creates a database holding details of students that she teaches. Complete each sentence with one term from the list. **[4 marks]**

| key field | integer | text | Boolean | OLE | currency |

a) The student's name has a data type of _____

b) Each student's enrolment number could be the _____

c) The field holding a passport photo would have a data type of _____

d) A field recording whether the term's fees are paid would have a data type of _____

2 A sports enthusiast has a database containing details of the winners of all the major tennis tournaments.

Give one reason for sorting the database.

Give one reason for searching the database **[2 marks]**

3 A clothes shop has a relational database. One table in the database has details of all the sales transactions it has made. The shop runs a loyalty card scheme and the details of its members are held in another table.

Suggest two reasons why the shop owner might want to link these two tables. **[2 marks]**

4 Here is a section of a database in a car showroom:

Registration	Make	Model	Colour	Built	Price $	Kilometres driven
ALZ 128	Ford	Fiesta	Red	1999	2,100	85,284
AHG 243	Opel	Corsa	Silver	1999	1,800	105,585
JFA 857	Ford	Mondeo	Grey	2005	4,250	74,728
BZE 439	Ford	Fiesta	Red	2000	2,000	100,031
CCA 876	Seat	Malaga	Red	2001	2,200	63,516
DZH 236	Fiat	Punto	Blue	2003	2,450	51,750
AVN 192	Opel	Corsa	Black	1999	1,750	115,658
ABD 439	Fiat	Panda	White	1998	1,000	65,432

The table is sorted into descending order of kilometres driven within alphabetical order of make. What is the new order of the eight registrations? **[3 marks]**

The systems life cycle (1)

The systems life cycle sets out the stages that take place during a system's development, its maturity and decline. This diagram illustrates the five stages of the cycle:

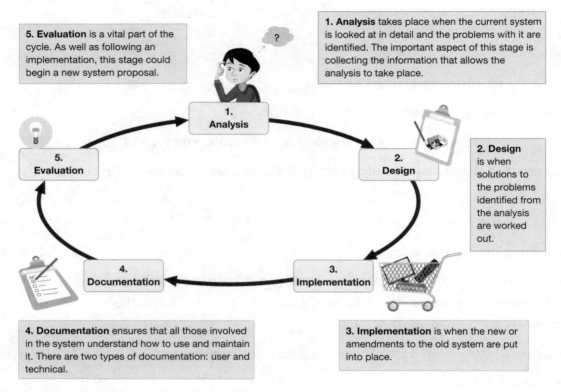

5. Evaluation is a vital part of the cycle. As well as following an implementation, this stage could begin a new system proposal.

1. Analysis takes place when the current system is looked at in detail and the problems with it are identified. The important aspect of this stage is collecting the information that allows the analysis to take place.

2. Design is when solutions to the problems identified from the analysis are worked out.

4. Documentation ensures that all those involved in the system understand how to use and maintain it. There are two types of documentation: user and technical.

3. Implementation is when the new or amendments to the old system are put into place.

Each stage involves specific tasks, but progress from one stage to another is not automatic. If requirements are not being met it may be necessary to return to a previous stage.

Analysis

This stage is carried out by a systems analyst and the major focus is on collecting data for analysing the current system. There are four ways of collecting information:

- interview key people who are directly involved in the system;
- observe the system as it works;
- issue questionnaires to all who are involved in the system;
- examine existing documentation that exists about the current system.

It is vital that all aspects of the current system are understood and properly recorded. Each of these information-collecting methods has advantages and disadvantages, especially regarding factors such as the number of people to contact and the number/depth of questions to ask. Make sure that you can discuss these methods.

Once as much information as time permits has been collected, it is presented as a report, the purpose of which is to fully describe the inputs, processing and outputs of the system.

The report will include a series of flowcharts showing the flow of information through the system as well as the connections and interdependences with other systems. It will highlight strengths to be built on and weaknesses that need solutions.

Arising from this analysis of the current system there will also be an outline of the requirements of the new system. The user will have particular needs, in terms of processes and outcomes, that will determine the information requirements, in terms of data that need to be input, processed and output by the new system.

Systems flowcharts are an important method of representing data flow through a system and are used at various stages in the cycle. There are five basic symbols used in a systems flowchart:

When this stage of the cycle is completed there is an understanding of the new system's requirements: its inputs, processing and output requirements. Additionally, there will be a proposal, with justification, for the hardware and software needs of the proposed system.

Design and development

The purpose of this stage is to create solutions for the proposed new system based on the report from the analysis stage, often resulting in a modular design.

At the end of this stage the systems analyst will have decided on the:

- hardware and software requirements;
- file structures and tables, including field names (and record keys), data types, table relationships;
- inputs and outputs, including data capture forms, **verification** and **validation** methods and rules, screen layouts, reports;
- module specifications using system flowcharts, data flow diagrams and pseudo code;
- relationships that exist between the different modules (and systems) in the organisation.

Verification is a method for checking data entry for transcription errors – the accuracy of the data entry. There are two methods: visual checks and double entry.

Validation is a software check that is used to ensure that the data that is being entered into the system can actually be used by the system. There are seven validation checks that the systems analyst can build into data input routines: range, length, character type, format, presence, consistency, check digit.

The **human–computer interface** (HCI), which refers to the way in which people actually use the system, also needs to be considered. The combination of input/output devices, the various data entry forms and the way that the system displays data are all vitally important to the success of the new system.

The systems analyst creates the HCI of the new system by careful design of all the elements that have been mentioned in this stage. In the same way,

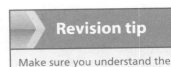

Make sure you understand the different validation methods.

you must be able to produce designs for the file structures, tables, data capture forms (including validation routines), screen layouts, and reports of a system.

The systems analyst will need to ensure that this development is carried out with careful attention to detail. Central to the design is the file/table structure. The system depends not only on the system storing the necessary information, but that the information is held in the correct format. The screen layouts, data capture forms and output reports need creating from the design proposals, ensuring that they work efficiently. Ensure that you are familiar with the process of creating these elements.

Quick test

Are the following statements true or false?

The system life cycle is a linear system.	
Questionnaires allow data to be collected from many people.	
HCI design considers the speed of data processing.	
Only a limited number of users will be interviewed.	
Verification tests whether input data can be used by the system.	
The systems analyst is only responsible for the analysis stage of the cycle.	

The systems life cycle (2)

Testing and implementation is the stage involving the creation of the system by the systems analyst, programmers and technicians. It needs to be built, thoroughly tested and then implemented – it becomes a 'live' system.

Testing

Each module of the system needs to be tested to see that it works as intended. Just as important as making sure each module works as intended, the systems analyst needs to make sure that the models work together as intended.

There are three important considerations:

- Data compatibility: is the output from one module usable by other connected modules?
- Hardware compatibility: in a supermarket, for example, do the proposed hand-held scanners work with the specially written software and the existing WiFi network?
- Memory and speed issues: an online booking system must not be flooded with requests prompting a 'denial of service' problem, nor can a supermarket system be allowed to crash because it cannot cope with the volume of transactions at checkouts.

To establish that the system responds as required, a comprehensive testing plan must be created. Data is needed that will test all the processing routines built into the software. There are four categories of test data: normal, live, extreme and abnormal.

It is important to remember that the testing phase may result in some processes or modules either not working as required, or not being efficient at a practical level. This will mean the systems analyst will have to redesign some of those processes and modules. This forces the cycle to pass back to the design and development stage.

Implementation

After the system has been thoroughly tested the next stage brings the new system into everyday use. Various strategies can be used to establish how the system goes live.

- Direct changeover: the old system is shut down and the new system is implemented immediately. The benefits of the new system are immediate but could result in massive data loss if it fails.
- Parallel running: the old and new systems are run alongside each other for a set period of time. If something fails, the old system is still running as a backup, but staffing costs are increased as two systems are running together.
- Pilot running: the new system is used in one area of the organisation until a decision is taken to implement it across the whole organisation. If the new system fails, only one area of the organisation is affected. This is more expensive than direct changeover because there needs to be an evaluation period before moving on to the next stage.

Revision tip

More detailed information about testing data models can be found in Collins Cambridge IGCSE ® ICT Student Book by Paul Clowrey and Colin Stobart (978-0-00-812097-9).

Revision tip

Make sure you can explain and give examples for the four categories of test data.

- Phased implementation: parts of the new system are gradually introduced. As one part is deemed to be successful, the next part is included. If one part fails, it is only that area that needs attention, but, as with pilot running, there needs to be an evaluation period before the next stages can be implemented.

Training will almost certainly be necessary for employees to become familiar with the new system. Employees may need to have time off to attend training or outside trainers could be brought into the organisation to train in situ. Some employees will find that their job responsibilities are reduced, others that theirs are enhanced. Some jobs may be lost but others such as hardware maintenance may be created.

Revision tip

Ensure that you can suggest a justifiable changeover method for a described situation.

Documentation

This supports the users and the managers of the system. Detailed documentation means that everyone will know what has taken place.

There are two types of documentation:

- Technical: describes the way the system was developed and how it works, its maintenance and operation. It will help analysts and programmers to make decisions about repairs, upgrades, updates and error checking. It contains: <u>purpose and scope of the system/program; hardware/software requirements</u>; details of file structure and field names; <u>input/output formats</u>; validation rules; notes on the programming language used; systems flowcharts/algorithms/program listing; <u>sample/test runs; details of known bugs/possible errors.</u>
- User: describes to the user how to load and use the system, offers help by way of tutorials and FAQs. It contains the <u>underlined</u> elements of the technical guide as well as: details of loading/installing/running the software; tutorials covering how to save a file, how to search, sort and print, how to add, delete and edit records; error handling routines and responses to FAQs; a trouble shooting guide/contact details/helpline details.

Revision tip

You will need to be able to identify the items of documentation that are specific to the technical or user documentation, and those which could be a part of either.

Evaluation

This actually takes place toward the end of each stage in the cycle, enabling the systems analyst to ensure that the system is developing as required. At the end of the entire development cycle there will be a full evaluation. This will take place at some significant point, such as once the system has been in use for a complete run of the organisation's natural business cycle. This might be after a month, six months or some other timeframe. An organisation needs to know if the new system is an efficient and appropriate solution to the problems that were identified and which set the whole process in motion. A comparison must be made between the new system and the one it has replaced. There should be a demonstrable improvement in the way tasks are carried out. The evaluation will also identify limitations and possible improvements to the system. Equally important are the views of the people who are using the new system.

Future developments

New systems can indicate that developments in other areas of the organisation are possible, or newer technology becomes available that makes previously unconsidered areas now worth investigating. The whole life cycle will begin again.

Quick test

Are the following statements true or false?

Direct changeover means that testing does not need to be done.	
Going 'live' is when the new system is finally operational.	
Employing new technology means that jobs are always lost.	
Phased implementation would be preferable for a complex system.	
A testing plan is needed to see if employees can operate the new system.	
Training and testing can be done at the same time.	

Exam-style practice questions

1. Validation and verification are two very different checking mechanisms. Describe each of these terms. State one difference between them. [2, 1 marks]

2. A data entry form is designed for a mechanic to log the vehicles that have been worked on during an eight-hour working day. (A vehicle licence plate has a minimum of 1 and a maximum of 8 alphanumeric characters.)

   Identify three items of data that may need to be entered into the form and for each of them give one item of normal data, extreme data and abnormal data that will be used to test that the data entered validates correctly. [3, 2, 2, 2 marks]

3. Identify and state the purpose of three items of technical documentation and two items of user documentation. [3, 2 marks]

4. Hannah's health food shop has just had a new computer system developed for stock control. It is a small business and Hannah is the only person who works there. What would be the best method of implementation? Give two reasons for your answer. [1, 2 marks]

5. A retail organisation is looking to radically change its stock control routines. The systems analysis team need to collect information about how the routines work now. There are 50 people working in this area of the organisation with three supervising personnel. Discuss the best ways for the team to gather the required information. [6 marks]

E-safety

The security of personal data when using internet-based systems is referred to as **e-safety**. Vast amounts of information are shared online through internet browsing, using email, social networking and online gaming, which provides an opportunity for criminal and inappropriate behaviour.

Personal data is any piece of information that uniquely identifies a person and should be kept private and confidential. Personal data will include: place and date of birth, passport details, addresses and telephone numbers. Many of these data items could be used for multiple purposes such as opening an online bank or shopping account, or applying for a passport. Children should be especially careful with the kind of information shared online as personal details are easily given, like school location or travel details, or favourite places to play with friends. In the hands of a **cyberbully** these items of information can lead to online abuse and even physical danger.

As highlighted in 'Commercial and ethical considerations', the internet is not regulated and anyone can create a website on any topic, so when browsing the internet extra care should be taken to ensure that the websites visited are reliable and trustworthy; check that your internet browsing software can be set to block certain sites; switch on the safe-search option within search engines; be aware that keywords entered into search engines can have more than one meaning.

Is there any indication that the website is part of a phishing scam? Is the website that is asking for credit card details secure? Websites with illegal material, whether pornographic, or spreading hate or xenophobic views, have an audience but should be squeezed out of hyperspace. Would a 'policed' internet work? Who would do the policing? Where would the organisation be based? Could all participating countries agree to a common set of standards? How much would it cost? Do laws already exist that could be applied? There are many advantages and disadvantages to controlling the internet that you need to consider.

Using email presents a number of problems and is a major source of virus infection and scams. To minimise risk consider: keeping contact lists updated to ensure known addresses are recognised; never opening email from an unknown source; never emailing personal details; always scanning attachments for viruses before opening them.

Spam is unsolicited electronic junk mail that attempts to lure the reader to a scam or infected website by clicking on a hyperlink. Email software often has anti-spam filters, some even 'learning' which emails are to be treated as spam.

Phishing involves an email that appears to come from a legitimate organisation such as a bank or law firm. Clicking on the included hyperlink may direct the user to a fake website where personal/login details are requested. Alternatively, personal information is requested in the phishing email.

This activity is starting to affect mobile phone users, with SMS messages being sent to users urgently requesting personal/login details. This is referred to as **smishing**. The voicemail equivalent is sometimes referred to as **vishing**.

These attempts to trick you into revealing personal data need to be identified and reported. Remember that an organisation will never simply contact you with a request that you reply to a message/visit a webpage in order to tell them personal data. Often the text of these requests have spelling mistakes, use bad grammar and appear to have been sent from a free web mail address, but many seem quite plausible. It is never wrong to be overly cautious. If you are suspicious then the scam can be reported to either the real organisation or to the police (www.actionfraud.police.uk).

Social networking sites are sources of vast amounts of personal data, shared or at least viewable by millions of users. To ensure that potential risks are avoided regularly check privacy settings, avoid clicking on unfamiliar links, provide minimal information in a profile, be cautious when making or accepting new friend requests.

Online gaming has grown tremendously in recent years, especially with the introduction of massively multiplayer online games (MMOGs). Many of these are set in make-believe worlds (World of Warcraft, League of Legends, Movie Star Planet, Club Penguin) and there is no need to share real information with other players, so create an avatar – a gaming character – for yourself. In some of these games, **VOIP** is available.

One of the features of social media, and the reason so many enjoy spending time on the sites, is the development of friendships and the ability to share and swop information so easily. These are also the aspects that cyberbullies and groomers exploit. It is very easy to overlook or forget strategies that minimise the dangers of inappropriate or accidental disclosure of personal data. Be suspicious of 'friends' wanting to move to private chat rooms, and of the language and requests sent via direct messaging. Know how to block and report users that are behaving inappropriately. Think carefully about how you interact with others on the internet and the way you use email, who you email and what to do with emails that arrive from someone you do not know. Above all always talk to an adult you trust whenever you feel that communication with someone is becoming inappropriate, or when someone has suggested meeting up.

> ### Revision tip
> Organisations such as banks will never send an email asking for personal/login details.

> ### Revision tip
> Never give personal details such as: your full name, your address, your mobile number, your email address, your school name; in other words, anything that could identify you. Never post a photograph of yourself wearing an identifiable school uniform, or of you outside your home where a number/street name is visible; in other words, anything that could locate you.

Quick test

Are the following statements true or false?

Email attachments are a major source of virus infection.	
Anti-spam filters can gradually learn which email messages are spam.	
Government departments always use phishing methods.	
Websites can only be set up and registered by legitimate organisations.	
Social networking sites provide a very safe environment for sharing personal information.	
An avatar is a make-believe character, whether a graphical image or a profile.	

The security of personal and commercial data

It is expected that companies and organisations that hold personal data, such as banks, hospitals, schools and government departments, provide very secure data protection.

When logging onto a website that uses confidential data it is important to know it is a genuine site. It is possible for someone to create a copy of a bank website (pharming) and then collect login details from people tricked into thinking it was the genuine website. A digital certificate is issued by the Certificate Authority to verify the identity of the owner. When an internet browser makes a secure connection to a banking website, for example, it checks the certificate and will display a warning should any issues or potential risks be identified.

It is vitally important to check that a webpage is secure before starting to disclose information such as credit card details. If the webpage is not secure then the transfer of data is not encrypted and the data can be read by anyone who intercepts it. More probably, if the webpage is not secure, it is not genuine and is probably part of a pharming exercise.

On sites such as banking or shopping, a little picture of a padlock should also be visible.

Trying to access a controlled system without permission or login details is **hacking**. A hacker will use a variety of methods to force their way into a system. The reasons for hacking are varied: curiosity; financial benefit; personal belief. The potential effects of hacking depend on the type of data and the system that has been hacked. The risk of having a system hacked is minimised by using strong firewalls and strong passwords. A firewall is an element of the network security system that monitors the data that is coming into your system or that is leaving it. A firewall also controls which applications on your computer can access the internet. This enables the system to be protected against unauthorised access.

Storing data in the cloud, and keeping it secure, is a concept that many users struggle with. Your data is stored at a remote location rather than on your own premises and you are handing its safeguarding over to a third party. Users worry about their data getting lost or wiped, corrupted or stolen, but storage providers, such as Dropbox, offer very sophisticated access procedures as well as encrypting techniques that are extremely secure.

Computer viruses are small self-replicating programs designed to invade a computer system, cause damage and to transfer to another computer. They can move or delete essential files, slow down a computer by using up memory and corrupt data files. The most common ways for a virus to infect a computer are by opening infected email attachments, downloading files from the internet or sharing files via a USB stick.

Revision tip

Users/customers need to ensure that they do as much as possible to ensure that passwords and other login data is kept secure. Many websites will require users to set a strong password when creating an account. Some organisations require that employees change their login password every six months. The use of anti-spyware software will also help to keep login details private.

Revision tip

The URL of a secure website will have https:// at the start, with the s indicating **secure**.

Revision tip

The only way to prevent an external hacking attempt is to have no external communications link of any kind, or simply to turn the equipment off.

Spyware is software that monitors and saves information about the user's internet activity, together with any data that has been typed in, probably including personal/login details. This information is transmitted to the originator of the spyware.

Pharming is another type of scam where a computer, infected by a virus, misdirects the computer to open a fraudulent website leading the user to think that they have gone to the actual website they were expecting. Once again personal/login details are what the pharmer or hacker is looking to collect.

Anti-virus software is system software designed to detect a virus and destroy or quarantine it. Sometimes destroying a virus carries the risk of it triggering some malicious process, so quarantining a virus isolates it where it cannot access or harm the rest of the system.

> **Revision tip**

Consider the actions that users can take to minimise the risks that online activity poses.

Quick test

Are the following statements true or false?

A picture of a lock beside a URL indicates the webpage is secure.	
Using a USB stick to save personal files will protect against virus infection.	
Hacking a website means to cause the website to crash.	
When your computer is plugged into the internet, data can be accessed by a hacker even if the computer is turned off.	
Anti-virus software is designed to detect and resolve virus attacks.	
Digital certificates are used to authenticate the owner of a website.	

Exam-style practice questions

1 Place a tick in the correct column to identify whether it would be OK to share the piece of personal information when using a social network. [3 marks]

	X	✓
School name		
First name		
Favourite meal		
Passport number		
Pet's name		

2 State two potential dangers that could arise from participating in online multi-player games. For each of these suggest a useful strategy to minimise the danger. [4 marks]

3 Distinguish between phishing and pharming. [1 mark]

4 Identity theft increased by 57 per cent between 2014 and 2015 according to figures collected by a UK fraud prevention service. Suggest reasons why social networking sites such as Facebook are the main sources of information for identity thieves. How can users of social networking sites minimise the risk of their information being stolen? [4, 2 marks]

Document layout

There are a number of elements to consider when thinking about the layout of a document: page size; its orientation; margins; columns; headers and footers. Additionally, there will be the question of defining and applying styles to headings, sub-headings and paragraphs.

The settings for layout can be applied at any time but it makes sense to sort this out before typing in any content because as new settings are applied this has an immediate effect on whatever content is present, possibly upsetting any spacing that has been used.

Paper size, orientation and margins can be selected as follows:

1. Layout tab

2. Page setup tag

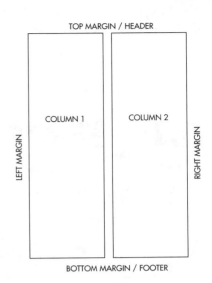

TOP MARGIN / HEADER

COLUMN 1   COLUMN 2

LEFT MARGIN   RIGHT MARGIN

BOTTOM MARGIN / FOOTER

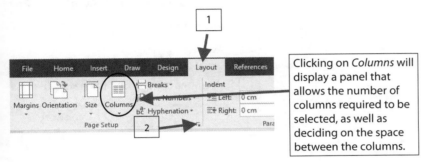

Clicking on *Columns* will display a panel that allows the number of columns required to be selected, as well as deciding on the space between the columns.

> ### Revision tip
>
> More detailed information about document layout and production can be found in *Collins Cambridge IGCSE ® ICT Student Book* by Paul Clowrey and Colin Stobart (978-0-00-812097-9).

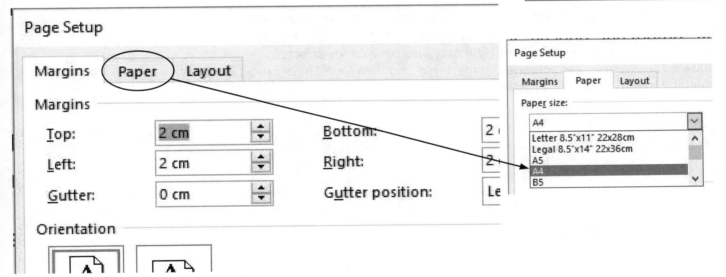

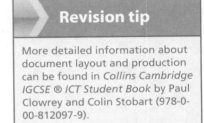

Information added into the header and footer areas will be displayed on every page of the document. As well as text and images that may form a title, other data such as the filename (and path), current date/time and page numbering can be included.

Footer

Tables are used to present information in a structured way. Each box in the table is called a cell. Row heights and column widths can be set separately. Cells in a row (horizontal) or column (vertical) can be merged. The text in a cell can be formatted in the same way as paragraph text. Cells can also contain images.

Highlight the cells needed to create the table, or choose to insert a table and specify the number of rows and columns

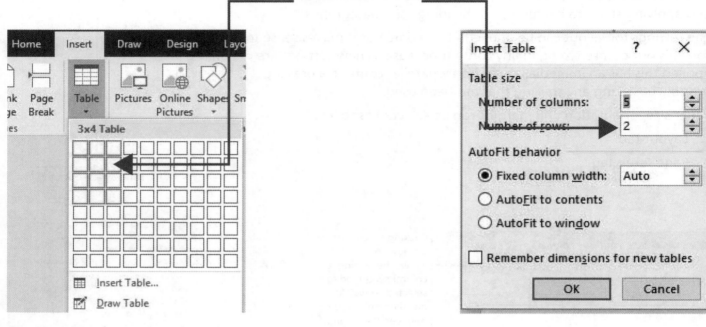

Document style

Style is a very important aspect of any document. The shape, colour and size of a font helps to reinforce the image and quality that the writer is attempting to convey. The font style may also have other effects added, for example: **emboldened**, <u>underlined</u> and *italicised*. These are all available through the font panel.

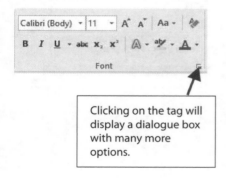

Clicking on the tag will display a dialogue box with many more options.

Creating a new style allows consistency across the whole of an organisation's documentation, and, when considering personal use, a simple way to apply a particular style to document content. This panel will be accessed from the collection of icons representing predefined styles, paragraphs or formatting.

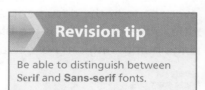

Clicking on the button *New style* at the bottom of the panel displays a dialogue box at which the font, size, colour and so on for the new style can be entered, along with an identifying name for the style and ensuring the style type is *paragraph*.

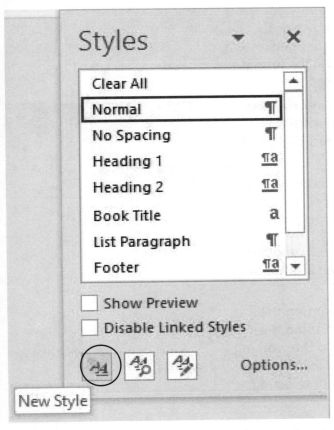

Once defined it is applied in the same way that text might be made **Bold** or $_{subscripted}$ – by selecting the style before typing content and then deselecting after typing, or highlighting the content already entered and then clicking on the style name in the displayed list.

Quick test

Are the following statements true or false?

It is more efficient to set page layout before entering content to a page.	
Columns always have fixed space between them.	
Page orientation is a style consideration.	
Font size is a layout consideration.	
To apply a style to text, highlight the text and select the style.	
Cell borders can have colours and styles applied.	

Document production (2)

File types

There are several file types that can be opened in or saved by word processing software. Sometimes material prepared by another person will require working on and it may have been saved in a generic file format – one that is recognised by a variety of application software.

Generic file types such as .csv, .rtf and .txt are used so that information can be widely shared, often between different application software such as results from a database search for inclusion in a word processed document.

Non-generic file types such as .doc, .docx, .pdf or .odt are formats created by particular application software.

Revision tip

Be confident describing the use and properties of different file types.

Document content

Some content for a word processed document may come from another source, such as the file types above, from webpages or even a file such as a .jpg image.

Copying text from another document is achieved by highlighting the text to be copied and then either clicking on the copy icon, using the Ctrl + C keys or selecting from an editing menu. Pasting into the working document is achieved by placing the cursor where the new text is to be placed and either clicking on the paste icon, using Ctrl + V or selecting paste from the editing menu.

Text from the internet, either from a webpage or from other documents viewed in a web browser, can be copied and pasted into a working document in the same way as from any other open text.

An image copied from a webpage needs to be saved into a folder on your computer first. With the cursor over the image to be copied right-click with the mouse to get a drop down menu which has 'Save picture as …' as an option. Once saved, the image is placed in your document by selecting 'Pictures' from the Insert menu/tab and then, in the dialogue box, navigating to the folder where you saved the image.

Revision tip

More detailed information about editing, positioning and adjusting images can be found in *Collins Cambridge IGCSE ® ICT Student Book* by Paul Clowrey and Colin Stobart (978-0-00-812097-9).

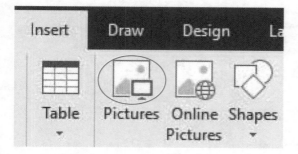

Charts and images can be copied and saved in exactly the same way.

Saving and printing

A document should be saved at regular intervals, perhaps after each paragraph has been written, or some significant element is completed. This ensures that you will always have a recent copy available should anything go wrong – software crashes, additional work/editing does not enhance the document or was incorrect. When 'Save as…' is selected the dialogue box will offer a range of file formats that your document can be saved as. The format you choose will depend on the purpose of the document, and who needs to work on it.

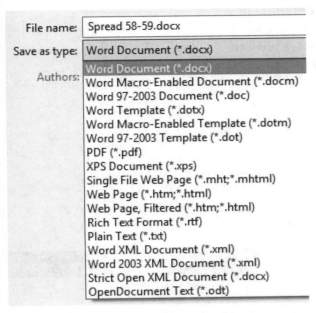

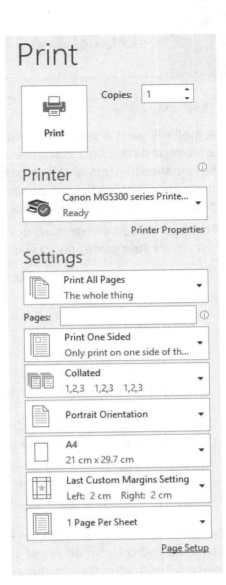

When printing a document there are a number of options but some will be limited by the capability of your printer and whether you have more than one printer on a network available. Clicking on the 'Printer Properties' link will open a dialogue box which is connected to the installed printer you have chosen from the selection available. Clicking on the 'Page Setup' link will open the dialogue box, as shown in the previous topic.

It is important to remember that any information/ images that you copy may be copyrighted material.

Quick test

Are the following statements true or false?

Text cannot be copied from a website.	
Generic file formats can be opened by a variety of application software.	
A .pdf file type is generic.	
An image from a webpage must be saved before you can copy it.	
A word processed document can be saved as a .csv file.	
Printing options depend on the installed printer.	

Document production (3)

Mail merge

A mail merge is a way of inserting data from a spreadsheet, database or a table of data into a word processed document. This is ideal for creating personalised letters or labels. Instead of editing an original letter several times to include different personalised information, the mail merge process will do this.

To create a mail merge, two documents are needed: a word processed document (template) and a file with the data for each letter.

A letter to be personalised may look like this:

Candidate's full name and address

details should go here

11 July 2016

Dear *candidate's first name*,

Thank you for your recent application for the position of Marketing Manager.

We have now had time to make calls to your referees and assess the development ideas for All Computers Inc. that you detailed. Your suggestions are very interesting and we are keen to talk to you about them.

We would be delighted if you could attend for interview at our offices on Digital Business Park on Thursday, 21 July 2016 at *Candidate interview time*.

Please confirm that you are able to attend by this Friday, 15 July 2016.

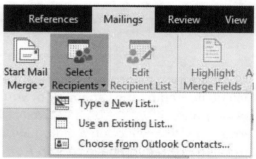

Text in black stays the same for each letter that is sent out. Text in *italic* are indicators/markers of where personalised information is to be placed. The text in *italic* is replaced with tags indicating a field name in the file containing the details. This document is then stored as the mail merge template.

To convert the letter to a template, the data file needs to be associated with it. Find the toolbar or menu that concerns mail merge, and 'Select Recipients', choosing to 'Use an existing list ...'

Having made this connection other icons in the toolbar become available, such as 'Edit Recipients'.

To place the 'tag' representing the candidate's first name after 'Dear' delete the *italic* text and leave the cursor there. Select the 'Insert Merge Field' icon to see the available fieldnames

from the data file. Click on *FirstName* to insert the tag in the letter.

«FirstName» «FamilyName»

«Street»

«Town»

«Post_Code»

The completed template would look like this:

11 July 2016

Dear «FirstName»,

Thank you for your recent application for the position of Marketing Manager.

We have now had time to make calls to your referees and assess the development ideas for All Computers Inc. that you detailed. Your suggestions are very interesting and we are keen to talk to you about them.

We would be delighted if you could attend for interview at our offices on Digital Business Park on Thursday, 21 July 2016 at «Interview».

After saving this template the actual mail merge can be carried out. There will be a 'Finish & Merge' icon in the toolbar. Choose to edit the documents to make sure that the letters are exactly as expected, before printing them. Once printed the letters are not usually saved. Saving the template with the merge fields is enough to allow the letter to be reproduced again if needed.

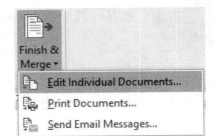

Proofreading

Spelling and grammar checks offer an immediate opportunity to correct mistakes but they do not catch every mistake. Spell checkers only alert you to words that are not spelt correctly, not whether the word used is the correct one. Once a document has been completed it needs to be proofread. This is the process of checking content and layout. Layout has to be consistent, so a check of the line and character spacing is needed, as well as a check for widows and orphans. It is often more useful if someone other than the original writer is the person who proofreads the document.

Revision tip

Know the difference between widows and orphans when discussing pagination.

Integrated documents

Often information from one application will be used in another. In chapters 9, 10 and 11 the idea of using different file types across different application software is explained and used in the practical exercises and examples. Documents that contain elements from other sources are integrated documents. Your evidence document is a good example of this as it may contain text, screenshot images, data exported from a database or HTML listings. A mail merge letter is also an integrated document.

Revision tip

It is important that the methods of transferring/copying/pasting/importing/exporting are fully understood.

Quick test

Are the following statements true or false?

Mail merging tools are usually found under the printing toolbar/menu.	
Proofreading, ideally, should not be done by the document author.	
Three files are needed for mail merging: original letter, template and data source.	
Special 'tags' are needed in a template to indicate where personal data is to be placed.	
It is recommended to edit mail merged documents before printing them.	
Proofreading is a check for factual accuracy.	
Integration involves combining components from different sources.	

Exam-style practice questions

You are a freelance travel writer and have been asked to prepare a short sample about the town of Ronda, 50 km inland of the Costa del Sol in southern Spain. You are submitting this to Compass Adventure Holidays.

The files you will need to use to work through these questions can be found at http://www.collins.co.uk/IGCSEICTrevision

Download: **Ronda v2.rtf, TempAndRain.rtf, NewBridge.jpg**

> Compass Adventure Holidays has a company style guide which contains the following relevant specifications:
>
> | | |
> |---|---|
> | Title | Sans-serif font, 18 point, dark blue, bold, centre aligned |
> | Subheading | Sans-serif font, 15 point, dark blue, bold, left aligned |
> | Body text | Serif font, 10 point, black, fully justified, 1.15 line spacing and 12 point after a paragraph |

1 Create a document in your word processing software called **EvidencePracticeWP**.

Your name should appear on every page of this document. You will need this document to place screenshot evidence of various tasks as you work your way through this exercise.

2 Using a suitable software package, load the file **Ronda v2.rtf** and save using the format of your software package as **CompassRonda**. [1 mark]

3 Set the page size to A4.
Set the left and right margins to 1cm and the top and bottom margins to 1.5cm.
Set the page orientation to landscape.
Evidence1. Place screenshot evidence of the settings in step 3 in **EvidencePracticeWP**. [1 mark]

4 Into the document header place:

- Your name

Into the document footer place two lines of text, each right-aligned:

- The text: **Date created** followed by today's date

- The text: **Date/time last printed** followed by an automated (updated) date and time field

   Make sure that these alignments match the page margins, and that the header and footer appear on each page. [2 marks]

5 Edit these paragraph styles to be applied to the text in the document. Refer to Compass Adventure Holidays' style guide for the details.
Title
Subheading
Body text
Evidence 2
Place screenshot evidence of your definition of the body text paragraph style in **EvidencePracticeWP**. [3 marks]

6 Format all the text into two equally spaced columns with a 2 cm gap between the columns. [2 marks]

7 At the start of the document enter the title: **The Fortress that became a Kingdom**.
Apply the title style to this text. [2 marks]

8 Apply the style body text to all the text below the title. [1 mark]

9 Apply the style subheading to each of the four subheadings. [1 mark]

10 In a new line above the subheading *History*, inset a new subheading: **Climate**.
Apply the style subheading to this new text. [2 marks]

11 Find the table **TempAndRain.rtf** and insert it between the subheadings *Climate* and *History*.
Make sure the table fits in the column width and apply the style body text to the text
in the table. [2 marks]

12 Centre align the month headings and the data for the months. [1 mark]

13 Embolden all the column and row labels. [1 mark]

14 Apply light grey (15–35 per cent) shading to the cells containing column and row labels. [1 mark]

15 Import the image **NewBridge.jpg** to be immediately below the heading *Location*.
Resize the image to about half the width of the column (approximately 6 cm),
maintaining the aspect ratio, and aligned with the left margin.
Apply text wrapping so that the body text flows around the image. [2 marks]

16 Spell check and proofread the document.
Place page breaks, if necessary, to ensure that:
- tables do not overlap two columns or pages;
- there are no blank pages;
- there are no widows or orphans. [2 marks]

17 Save and print your document.
Evidence 3
Make sure that your name is printed on each page of your document.
To check your work, download the completed version of this, **CompassRonda v2.pdf**,
and the evidence document **EvidencePracticalWP.pdf**

Total marks available: 24

Data analysis (1)

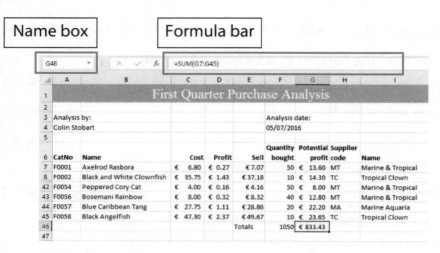

Layout and content

A spreadsheet is a grid made up of a number of cells which are referenced by the column letter and row number. In this example rows 9–41 are hidden.

The cell with the highlighted border, cell G46, is the active cell – where the next typed content will be placed. The name box identifies which is the current active cell. The formula bar is where the contents of a cell are displayed and can be edited.

Cells can:

- contain a number, a text label, or a formula/function:
  cell B7 has a text label, F7 has a number and G46 has a function (look at the formula bar to see its content, =sum(G7:G45), the result is displayed in the cell, 833.43);
- be formatted: cell C7 is formatted to currency (€) and 2 decimal places, F4 has a date in dd/mm/yyyy format;
- have content in different font typefaces, colours, sizes and styles just as in a word processed document – row 6 has all text in **bold**, the text in row 1 has a serif font typeface and is larger than the sans-serif font used in the rest of the spreadsheet;
- be shaded, as in row 1, and have styles given to their borders.

File types

Data that is going to be loaded into a variety of spreadsheet software is often presented in .csv (comma separated variable) format, which is basically a file of plain text and can be opened by any spreadsheet application. It is very important that after any editing has taken place in the spreadsheet it is saved as a spreadsheet (with file extensions such as .xls, .xlsx, .sxc or .ods). This is because if the spreadsheet were resaved as a .csv file all formatting and formulae/functions would be lost.

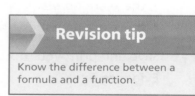

Revision tip

Know the difference between a formula and a function.

Functions

There are a vast number of available functions and their workings can be very complex. At a minimum you should familiarise yourself and be confident working with these functions:

Function (parameter)	Comments and similar/connected functions
=average(range)	Finds the average value over a range of cells.
=count(range)	Range of cells to count if there are numbers in them. Also counta() and countif().
=if(what is being tested, what to do if true, what to do if false)	Often nested together to test multiple conditions.
=max(range)	Finds a maximum value of a range of data. Also min().
=round(value to round, number of decimal places to display)	Rounds a value. Also rounddown(), roundup(), int().
=sum(range)	Finds the total over a range of values. Also sumif().
=vlookup(what to find, where to look, what to return)	looks for value in a table and returns another value from the table. Also hlookup().

Absolute and relative references

Functions and formulae are very often replicated across a number of cells. When this is done the formulae and functions automatically adjust cell references to reflect the new row/column that it is pasted into. This is called relative referencing. To make a cell reference remain exactly the same during replication, an absolute cell reference is needed. This is achieved by putting a $ sign in front of the column and the row reference – C7 (relative) would become $C$7 (absolute).

Quick test

Are the following statements true or false?

There is no difference between functions and formulae.	
=counta(range) will count all the cells with alphabetic characters in them.	
Using absolute referencing ensures cell references remain unchanged during replication.	
Cell contents can be edited in the formula bar.	
=sum(G7:G45) adds together the content of cell G7 and G45.	
Saving a spreadsheet as a .csv file does not preserve formatting or formulae.	

Data analysis (2)

Example functions and formulae

Go to the webpage www.collins.co.uk/IGCSEICTrevision and download DepartmentStore.csv.

Open the file in your spreadsheet software and then save it as a spreadsheet.

The spreadsheet is incomplete and has functions and formulae displayed as text. For each of the cells that have a function or formula add '=', an equals sign, to the front so that, for example, cell E2 will contain =VLOOK UP(LEFT(A2,1),$A$33:$B$40,2, FALSE), but displays 'Bedding'.

Having converted the text functions and formulae so that they work, replicate the functions and formulae in:

- E2, G2, H2 and I2 down through rows 3 to 26;
- F27 across columns G to I;
- E33 down through rows 34 to 40.

Apply formatting, for example to cells that display currency. Other effects, such as shading and border styles, can also be added.

Save the spreadsheet.

After adding formatting to some cells the spreadsheet could look like this – note that some rows here have been hidden.

	A	B	C	D	E	F	G	H	I
1	Salesman ID	First name	Family name	Gender	Department	Monthly sales	Commission	Bonus payment	Total extra
2	B3650	Lachelle	Ravenscroft	F	Bedding	$ 6,180.00	$ 123.60	$ 61.80	$ 185.40
3	B5986	Dario	Moris	M	Bedding	$ 6,256.00	$ 125.12	$ 62.56	$ 187.68
23	S7990	Dale	Huck	M	Sportswear	$ 6,959.00	$ 146.13	$ 69.59	$ 215.72
24	T8936	Jon	Pool	M	Textiles	$ 4,825.00	$ 96.50	$ 24.13	$ 120.63
25	T9438	Mario	Ashworth	M	Textiles	$ 6,303.00	$ 126.06	$ 63.03	$ 189.09
26	T9782	Johnette	Dobrowolski	F	Textiles	$ 6,123.00	$ 122.46	$ 61.23	$ 183.69
27						$ 154,811.00	$ 2,848.53	$ 1,341.97	$ 4,190.50
28			Male	10					
29			Female	15					
30									
31									
32	Departments		Commission		Total extra				
33	B	Bedding	0.02		$ 806.04				
38	M	Menswear	0.012		$ 894.88				
39	S	Sportswear	0.021		$ 423.57				
40	T	Textiles	0.02		$ 493.41				
41					$ 4,190.50				

Carefully study the functions that you have created and applied, making sure that you are comfortable with the syntax and the elements used to make the returned results. Within the spreadsheet the following have been used, either by themselves or in combination (nested):

- cell E2: VLOOKUP, LEFT
- cell G2: ROUNDDOWN, VLOOKUP
- cell H2: IF
- cell F27: SUM
- cell D28: COUNTIF
- cell E33: SUMIF

Cell H2 contains a formula.

Consider how you would add functions to find the maximum, minimum and average monthly sales.

Charts

Once data has been summarised it is usual for charts to be created. A bar or pie chart would be suitable here to show 'Total extra' for each department.

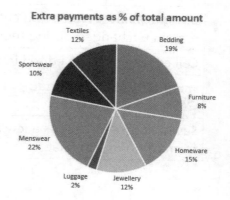

Extra payments as % of total amount

Using your spreadsheet software explore the different charts that are possible and how the various elements in the chart can be formatted/personalised. It is possible to create charts from data that are not physically adjacent to each other, for example, in these cases from columns B and E. These charts are dynamic – as data in the spreadsheet changes so will the charts.

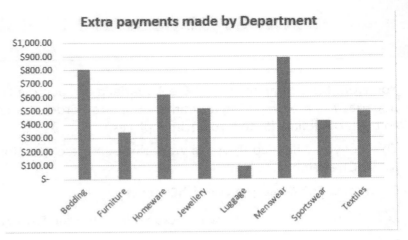

Extra payments made by Department

Charts can be copied and pasted into other documents.

Printing and saving

When printing spreadsheets ensure that the information printed is readable. Sometimes if the option 'Fit to print one page' (under the 'Page' tab) is used with large spreadsheets, the resulting printout is very difficult to read – maybe changing the page orientation improves this.

Printing gridlines, along with row and column headings, is often very helpful, enabling you to see exactly which cells have been used.

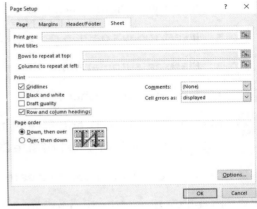

Headers and footers can be attached to a spreadsheet which will be printed on every printed page.

As well as printing a spreadsheet showing its values, you will need to be able to print out the spreadsheet showing the functions and formulae used. To switch from viewing values to viewing formulae press CTRL + ` or look for an option such as:

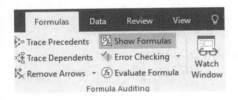

Quick test

Are the following statements true or false?

Statement	
=LEFT(A2,1) examines the left-most single character in cell a2.	
In formula view cell contents are always fully visible.	
To create a chart, data must be in adjacent cells.	
=VLOOKUP(A2,$A$33:$B$40,2, FALSE) returns a value in the second column of the lookup array.	
Headers and footers appear at the very top and very bottom of the spreadsheet only.	
'Fit to 1 page' can cause printing to be too small to read.	

Revision tip

When printing out a spreadsheet in formulae view it is vital to ensure that the entire contents of cells are visible.

Revision tip

More detailed information about producing graphs and charts can be found in *Collins Cambridge IGCSE ® ICT Student Book* by Paul Clowrey and Colin Stobart (978-0-00-812097-9).

Exam-style practice questions

You work for a company called Eze Aquaria, a company selling freshwater and marine fish for small aquaria. You are preparing a summary of placed orders for the Purchasing Manager. All currency values are to be in US dollars ($) to two decimal places.

The files you will need to use to work through these questions can be found at http://www.collins.co.uk/IGCSEICTrevision

Download: **FishCataogue.csv**, **FishOrder.csv**.

1 Using a suitable software package, load the file **FishOrder.csv**.

- Insert your name in cell B3.

- Insert today's date in cell B4.

- Place an automated file name (with path) in the footer.

- Save as a spreadsheet. [1 mark]

2 Merge cells A1 to H1 and format the merged cell to have a dark grey background, with white serif font text of size 20 point. [1 mark]

3 Use the cells A48 to B52 to create a named range called **Suppliers**. [2 marks]

4 In cell C7 use a function to lookup the *Cost* of a fish. Use the *CatNo* as the single lookup value and the file **FishCatalogue.csv** for the array. The function must include both absolute and relative referencing but must not include a named range. [4 marks]

5 The *Total* cost of buying a fish (in cell E7) is its *Cost* multiplied by the *Quantity* ordered. Enter a formula to display this. [1 mark]

6 The *Name* of a supplier (in cell G7) is found by using the *Supplier code* in a lookup function which references the named range *Suppliers*. Enter the function to display the supplier name. [4 marks]

7 Replicate the functions/formulae created in steps 4, 5 and 6 for each fish in the list. [1 mark]

8 In cell D48 use a function to count the number of orders from each of the suppliers. Use *Supplier code* as the criterion. [3 marks]

9 In cell E48 use a function to total the *Total* for each of the Suppliers. Use *Suppliers code* as the single criterion with the fish *Supplier codes* as the range to be examined and totalling the fish *Total*. The function must include both absolute and relative referencing but must not include a named range. [4 marks]

10 In cell F48 use a formula to work out the amount of discount that can be claimed based on the number of orders and their value:

If *Orders* > 4 and then

If *Value* > $15000 then 0·1 is claimed, otherwise 0·07

If *Orders* < 5 and then

If *Value* > $15000 then 0·05 is claimed, otherwise 0. [5 marks]

11 In cell G48 enter a formula to multiply *Value* by *Discount claimed*. [1 mark]

12 In cell H48 enter a formula to subtract *Discount claimed* from *Value* [1 mark]

13 Replicate the functions/formulae created in steps 8, 9, 10, 11 and 12 for each supplier in the list. [1 mark]

14 Enter a function into cells E45, D53, E53, G53 and H53 to total the values immediately above them. [1 mark]

15 Format cells F48 to F52 as percentage. [1 mark]

16 Make all column headings and labels bold. [1 mark]

17 Right align any heading that appears over numeric data. [1 mark]

18 Save the spreadsheet.

19 **Printout 1**

Hide rows 11–40.

Print out a copy of the analysis showing values. Make sure that:

- it is in landscape orientation;

- row and column headings are displayed;

- the printout fits to a single page;

- the contents of all cells are fully visible. [4 marks]

20 **Printout 2**

Unhide rows 11–40.

Print out a copy of the spreadsheet showing formulae. Make sure that:

- it is in landscape orientation fitting to 2 pages wide;

- row and column headings are displayed;

- the contents of all cells are fully visible. [3 marks]

Total marks available: 40. The solutions, Printouts 1 (**Tropical1.pdf**) and 2 (**Tropical2.pdf**), can be downloaded from the webpage.

Presentations (1)

Presentation software is commonly used to present ideas to large audiences. Each page within a presentation is referred to as a slide. Slides can contain text, images, links to video clips and sound files, and animation. The sequence in the way and timing that these elements are displayed can be controlled by a mouse click or automatic timing.

Presentations can be printed out, as an audience copy with the slides arranged on the page to enable note-taking, or with content notes as an aid for the presenter.

Layout and terminology

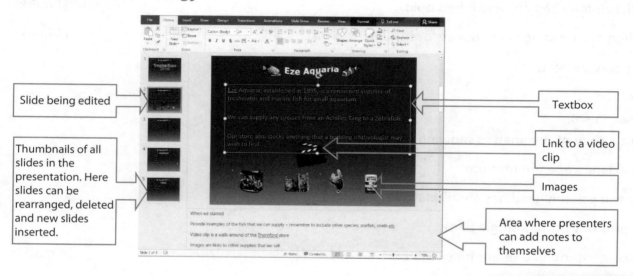

Large organisations will have a house style, and all presentation slides may need to have a particular layout with text and graphics always appearing in the same positions. This is achieved by having a **master slide**, a template that is used do define the layout style, which is then the basis of all the slides in the presentation. The layout of the master slide for Eze Aquaria can be seen in the screenshot where the third slide has yet to have content added to it.

Any elements on a slide can have animation applied to them – affecting how that element appears on the slide. When the element is clicked on, the options in the Animations menu become available.

Movement effects between slides is called transition.

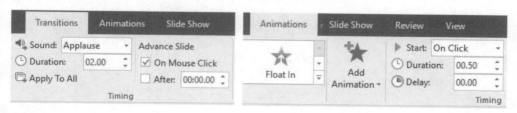

Creating a new presentation

Once a blank presentation has been opened it is possible to select the type of layout required for each slide that is added. You do not have to choose one of these – they are time-savers, and the same effects can be achieved manually. Each slide can have its own particular layout and mix of elements.

To place an element on a slide, whether a text box, graphic, video clip or anything else, there is an icon for that element under the Insert tab.

As well as opening a blank presentation, it is possible to start a new presentation by opening another file type that contains the information

required. For example, simple text files (.txt or .rtf) containing titles and content can be loaded into slides by selecting **New slide** → **Slides from outline**.

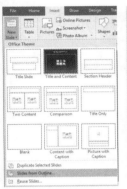   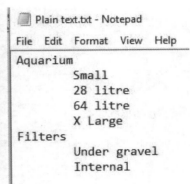

Headers and footers are available on presentation slides and appear just as they do in a word processed document or a spreadsheet. To take effect they need to be placed on the master slide.

Quick test

Are the following statements true or false?

A presentation consists of a number of slides.	
The special effect added to an element on a slide is called transition.	
New content can be added to slides from an external file by choosing 'Text box' under the insert tab.	
A footer appears on every slide because it is set up on the master slide.	
Presenter notes can be printed out alongside the slide they refer to.	
Once a slide layout has been chosen, every slide in the presentation takes the same layout.	

Inserting/creating charts

An already created chart, such as a pie or bar chart, can be copied and pasted from another application, or it can be created with the presentation software itself.

Clicking on Chart under the Insert tab will present a dialogue box asking you to choose the type of chart to create – a list similar to what you would find in a spreadsheet application. A small spreadsheet-like window opens with some pre-inserted data in it, together with the requested chart type illustrated using that data. It is possible to copy and paste data from a spreadsheet into this small spreadsheet, or you could type in the data directly. Once the data is entered, the spreadsheet window can be closed and the chart formatted as required.

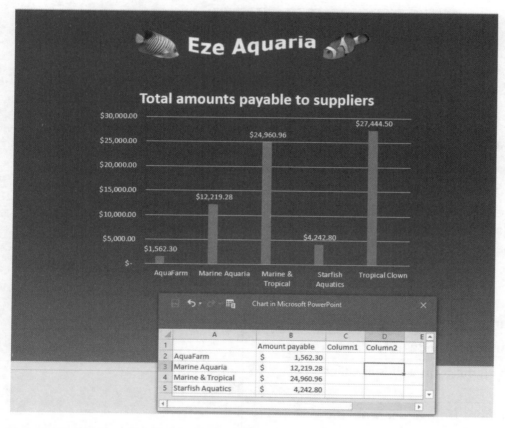

Finalising and displaying the presentation

The way a presentation runs will depend on how the elements on each slide are set to appear and how the sides are set to transition.

This can all be done automatically if all the animations and transitions are set with timing delays. This is perfect for a promotional presentation that may be required to run, for example, at an exhibition or museum.

If the presentation is to be used by a speaker then elements on individual slides may be set to appear/move on with the click of the presenter's handheld wireless mouse/pointing device. This makes the presentation more effective, as the presenter is driving the pace and delivery of the presentation. Additionally, the audience may need to have a copy of the presentation slides, printed as handouts, with space alongside for them to add notes. Look for printer options such as these:

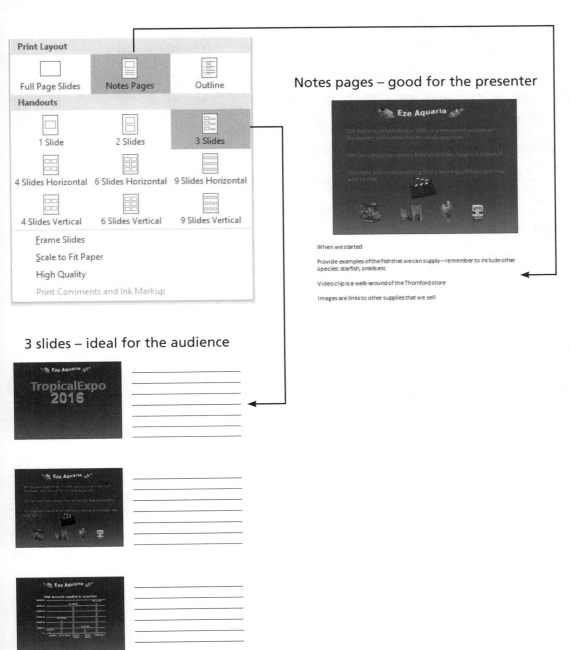

Notes pages – good for the presenter

3 slides – ideal for the audience

Quick test

Are the following statements true or false?

Charts can only be pasted in after being completed in other application software.	
Transition between slides is always based on time settings.	
Animation of elements can be automatic or manual.	
Audience members can have copies of the presentation as a handout.	

Exam-style practice questions

You are going to prepare a presentation for the Financial Director of Eze Aquaria.

The files you will need to use to work through these questions can be found at http://www.collins.co.uk/IGCSEICTrevision. Download: **Banner.jpg**, **1516EAPres.rtf**, **1516AEpres.csv**, **1516NetOrders.rtf**.

1 Using a suitable software package open: **1516EAPres.rtf**.
Make sure that there are only three slides, a title page plus two containing a title and some text. Save the presentation. [3 marks]

2 Eze Aquaria has a house style that includes the following:

- background colour for slides is referenced with the hexadecimal of #023286, or RGB of 2, 50, 134;

- Banner.jpg is displayed across the top of each slide;

- title text: 44 point, light blue, sans-serif font;

- first level text: 24 point, orange, sans-serif font;

- footer detail: 16 point, white, serif font.

Apply these house rules to the master slide.
Place your name in the left of the footer and an automatic date stamp in the right of the footer. These are to be the only details in the footer. [4 marks]

3 Apply this master layout to the three slides in the presentation.
Slide 1 is a title slide. Adjust font size to 60 point for the title and 35 point for the subheading, both centred. [2 marks]

4 A pie chart is needed on slide 2. The information is in **1516AEpres.csv**. [2 marks]

5 Slide 3 requires a table of information. The information is in **1516NetOrders.rtf**. [2 marks]

6 Save the presentation. [2 marks]

7 The Financial Director requires each member of the audience to have a copy of the presentation with room alongside each slide image to write notes.
Print the audience copy. [1 mark]

Total marks available: 14. The solutions, the completed presentation and the handout copy, can be downloaded from the webpage: **www.collins.co.uk/IGCSEICTrevision**

Data manipulation (1)

The terminology and structure of databases is explained in Chapter 6 and it is recommended that you revise these pages before working on the practical aspects here.

The files you will need to use to work through these examples can be found at http://www.collins.co.uk/IGCSEICTrevision.

Download: **Banknotes.csv** and **Chief Cashiers.csv**.

Loading data and assigning data types

Open Banknotes.csv in your database software. This will be through an 'External data' or 'Data import' tab/menu. As a .csv file the file type to import is a *Text File* and not a spreadsheet file. The file is a comma delimited file, the first row of data contains field names and PickNo is the primary key.

Your database should now have one table called Banknotes. The fields have names but it is important to make sure that they have the correct data type assigned to them. Edit the record structure so that the fields are as shown.

Date should be set to **Date/Time** with **Short date** (dd/mm/yyyy).

Banknotes	
Field Name	**Data Type**
PickNo	Short Text
Date	Date/Time
Cashier	Short Text
Denomination	Short Text
Colour	Short Text
Replacement	Yes/No
Condition	Short Text
Value	Currency

Replacement should be set to **Yes/No** with format **True/False** and displayed as **Checkbox**.

Value should be set to **Currency** as **Euros** with **0** decimal places.

The first few records in the table should look like this:

Banknotes							
PickNo ▾	Date ▾	Cashier ▾	Denomination ▾	Colour ▾	Replacement ▾	Condition ▾	Value ▾
B210	22/11/1928	Mahon	10 Shillings	Red Brown	☐	VF	€130
B212	22/11/1928	Mahon	1 Pound	Green	☐	VF	€60
B223	15/07/1930	Catterns	10 Shillings	Red Brown	☐	EF	€100
B225	15/07/1930	Catterns	1 Pound	Green	☐	VF	€25

The first record with a tick in the Replacement field is B250. In the table there are 45 records with each record having 8 fields.

It is possible to create a record structure before introducing data to it. Data can then be imported (appended) into that 'empty' but already structured table. It is very important to check that the data being imported shares exactly the same structure as the empty table. Data can also be manually entered into the empty table.

> ### Revision tip
>
> After loading up the records into a table it is a good idea to spend a few moments moving between the design and datasheet views to make sure that the changes you have made do actually display data as needed.

Creating relationships between tables

For there to be a relationship between tables, another table is needed. Load the data in **ChiefCashiers.csv** into your database as second table. It is a comma delimited file, the first row contains field names, FamilyName is the primary key.

The first few records in the table should look like this.

FamilyName ▾	FirstName ▾	BankStart ▾	CashierStart ▾	CashierEnd ▾
Bailey	Andrew	1985	2004	2011
Beale	Percival	1924	1949	1955
Catterns	Basil	1908	1929	1934
Cleland	Victoria	1996	2014	
Fforde	John	1957	1966	1970

Victoria Clelend is still the Chief Cashier, which is why there is no date in the field CashierEnd.

The table has 17 records and each record has 5 fields.

To create a relationship between tables a panel must be opened that allows you to view and create relationships.

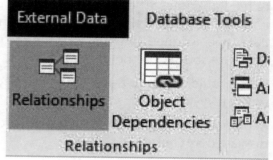

Connect *Cashier* to *FamilyName*. This creates a one-to-many relationship between the two tables. *Cashier* is a foreign key in the table Banknotes. There is one ChiefCashier's name on many Banknotes.

Once the relationship has been created, look at the table ChiefCashier and click on the little icon beside the Cashier's FamilyName and the Banknotes connected to that Cashier are displayed.

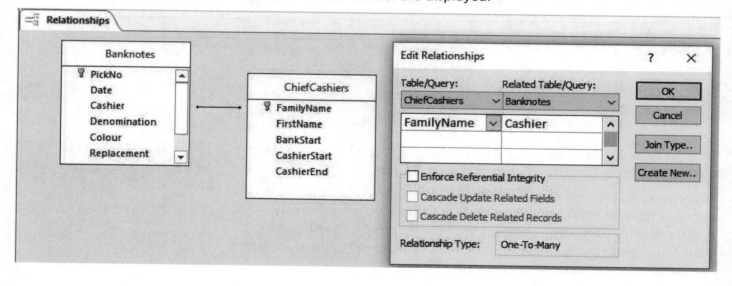

⊞ Harvey	Ernest	1885	1918	1925	
⊟ Mahon	Cyril	1901	1925	1929	

PickNo ▾	Date ▾	Denomination ▾	Colour ▾	Replacement ▾	Condition ▾	Value ▾
B210	22/11/1928	10 Shillings	Red Brown	☐	VF	€130
B212	22/11/1928	1 Pound	Green	☐	VF	€60
✱				☐		

Quick test

Are the following statements true or false?

In a one-to-many-relationship, the 'one' represents the foreign key.	
In a .csv file, commas separate each of the data items.	
In a record structure, a small icon identifies the field that is the primary key.	
Record structures must be created before data is imported into the table.	
In the image of the *ChiefCashiers* table above, the three numerical fields have a data type of date.	
Connections between tables are relationships.	

Data manipulation (2)

Sorting, filters and queries

Sorting data puts the whole data set into a different order. Click in the field to sort first and use the AZ↓ and ZA↓ buttons. Only a single order can be applied, such as by *Value*. It would not be possible to sort into *Condition* within *Cashier* – a query would need to be created for this.

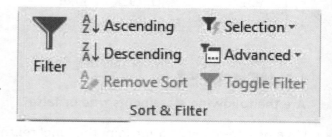

Filtering and querying produces a subset of the data that fits the search criteria. Filtering will display the whole record. Click in the field and then the Filter (or Advanced) button to be asked what the filter criteria is.

With a **query** it is possible to specify particular fields from a record to display. Choose Query Design to be able to specify the table and fields to use and display, and the criteria to be applied. Queries can also be saved.

Use the Run button to apply the query.

In a query you can use wildcards, with '?' representing one character and '*' representing many characters.

For example, in this query, a selection of fields from records in the Banknote table will be displayed when the Cahier is Peppiatt **or** Beale **and** when the Condition for either Cashier is VF or EF. Details of 14 banknotes are displayed.

Field:	PickNo	Date	Cashier	Denomination	Condition
Table:	Banknotes	Banknotes	Banknotes	Banknotes	Banknotes
Sort:	Ascending				
Show:	☑	☑	☑	☑	☑
Criteria:			"Peppiatt"		Like "?F"
or:			"Beale"		Like "?f"

In the above query you can see that the field 'PickNo' is going to be used to sort the records that are returned for the query into ascending order. In the same way the records could be sorted according to the descending order of a field. Multiple sort criteria can be applied in a query. For example the below query shows that the returned records will be sorted firstly into ascending order of 'Condition' and then descending 'PickNo' order within 'Condition'. This image also shows that, in *MS Access*, the precedence of the instructions are taken as left to right, 'Condition' and then 'PickNo'. Within a report, the order that records are presented can be effected in two ways. When the report is created the order of the records can be specified either in the report's setup or by attaching a query that already specifies the record order.

Revision tip

Be sure to know the difference between a filter and a query.

Field:	Date	Cashier	Denomination	Condition	PickNo
Table:	Banknotes	Banknotes	Banknotes	Banknotes	Banknotes
Sort:				Ascending	Descending
Show:	☑	☑	☑	☑	☑
Criteria:		"Peppiatt"		Like "?F"	
or:		"Beale"		Like "?f"	

Data entry forms

In an organisational setting, data would be entered into a table through a data entry form.

Look for a panel or menu that allows the creation of a form.

The Form Wizard is the simplest way to create a form. Select the table that the form will be connected to and the fields in that table to be used. Using the table **Banknote** and using **all** the fields in the record will give something similar to the form shown on the right.

Notice the use of white space (the areas that are 'empty') that surround the field names and the data fields. It aids the readability of the form, freeing it of distracting clutter. Care should be taken when choosing the font styles and sizes to ensure it is readable – especially important if the form is accessed via a smartphone or other small screen. The spacing and position of the field names and data fields should be carefully thought through, because the way data is presented should make sense – there may be a logical sequence to the way data is presented and, again, it needs to be comfortably readable.

Use the available design tools to edit and create a more user-friendly form. For example, you could add **drop-down lists** for the available *Denominations*, *Cashier* name and *Condition*. *Replacement* could be changed for two radio buttons (sometimes called option buttons) in an **option group** which are titled Yes and No.

Replacement

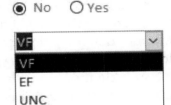

Condition

Alternatively, a **validation** routine could have been added to *Condition* to ensure that only one of the three permitted conditions is entered.

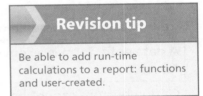

Reports

When starting to create a report, the choice of connecting a table (displaying the whole data set of a table, sorted on one field) or a saved query (displaying a subset which fulfils certain criteria) is given.

It is important to distinguish between the various parts of a report:

- Report Header: only printed at the start of the report's first page – the title;
- Page Header: printed at the top of every page – the headings of the columns;
- Detail: the body of the page, listing individual records;
- Page Footer: printed at the foot of every page – today's date/time and page numbering;
- Report Footer: printed after the last detail line on the final page of the report.

In this example, the Report Footer contains a **run-time created field**, count(), which prints the number of printed records by counting the number of PickNo.

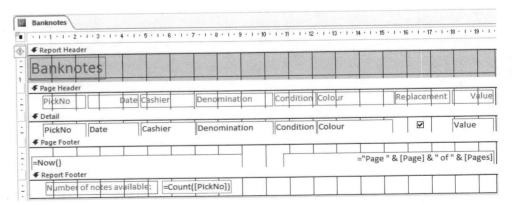

The profit of a product (sales price – cost price) might be a data item that needs adding to a report, query or a form. This is achieved by adding an 'unbound' textbox which contains, for example =[SalesPrice]-[CostPrice]. It is more efficient to have this calculated at run-time rather than stored as a separate field in the product's record. Field content can be added, multiplied, divided, summed, counted, averaged and examined for maximum and minimum values. You will need to check the syntax of the of these functions before using them.

An important consideration is the report's layout. Records can be displayed in a variety of ways: tabular, columnar, as labels. You need to experiment with the available layouts that your software offers. The alignment of data may also need adjusting, for example should column headings be centred? Should some data labels be right aligned? How many decimal places need displaying for currency?

At times some data in a report needs to be hidden. Although this sounds strange, if a displayed field is calculated at run-time, the data fields in the calculation have to be part of the report. However, you may only need the resulting calculation to be viewed, in which case you have the option for the data field to be hidden (invisible).

Sometimes data from a database needs to be used in other software. For example, a summary of the values of banknotes held for each cashier may need to be used in a spreadsheet, or a count of the number of different denominations might be needed in a table in a word processed document. In these cases, you will need to export data from the database in a suitable format such as .rtf or .csv. Note that you can read a database table from MS Access straight into MS Excel.

Quick test

Are the following statements true or false?

A data entry form is a common way of entering data to a table.	
Option buttons cannot be used to select 'Male', 'Female'.	
Run-time created fields are not fields stored in a record.	
Table data can be sorted into multiple orders.	
Wildcards are alternative substitutes for particular characters.	
Queries need to be recreated before they can be re-applied.	

Exam-style practice questions

You are a collector of English banknotes buying and selling through online auctions. You are going to create, and work with, a database of banknotes that you currently have for sale.

The files you will need to use to work through these questions can be found at http://www.collins.co.uk/IGCSEICTrevision.

Download: **BanknoteSale.csv, ChiefCashiers.csv**.

1 Create a document in your word processing software called **EvidencePracticeDatabase**.

Your name should appear on every page of this document.

You will need this document to place screenshot evidence of carrying out various tasks as you work your way through this exercise.

2 Using a suitable software package import the file **BanknotesSale.csv**.

Use these field names and data types:

	PickNo	Text	Cataloguing reference number
Serial	Text	Banknote serial number	
Date	Date	Short date. Print date of the banknote	
Cashier	Text	Family name of the Bank of England Chief Cashier	
Denomination	Text	Face value of the banknote	
Colour	Text	Predominant colouring	
Replacement	Boolean	Display in report as Yes/No only	
Condition	Text	Code for general condition	
Value	Currency	Sale price, Euros, 2 decimal places	

Set *Serial* as the primary key field

[5 marks]

3 Import **ChiefCashiers.csv** as a new table in your database, setting *FamilyName* as the primary key field.

Evidence 1. Take screenshot evidence showing the field names and data types used in the two tables and insert into your evidence document.

[1 mark]

4 Create a one-to-many relationship as a link between the *FamilyName* field in the *ChiefCashier* table and the *Cashier* field in the *BanknoteSale* table.

Evidence 2. Take screenshot evidence showing the relationship between the two tables and insert into your evidence document.

[1 mark]

5 Produce a report that:

- contains a new field called **ExhibitionPrice** which is calculated at run time. This is 85 per cent of *Price*;

- shows only the records where *Replacement* is No;

- has the data sorted into ascending order of *PickNo*; within alphabetical order of the Cashier's *FamilyName*;

- shows *FirstName* and *FamilyName* from the *ChiefCashier* table and then the *PickNo, Serial, Date* and *Condition* from the *BanknoteSale* table followed by the run-time field *ExhibitionPrice* with labels and data fully visible;

- fits on a single portrait page;

- calculates the number of banknotes in the report, with a suitable label, placed as the last line of the report;

- has a heading **Dorset Notaphilist Trade Fair – prices**;

- has your name in the page footer. [9 marks]

6 Save and print the report. [1 mark]

7 A collector has emailed you for a listing of all the available 10 shillings and replacement one pound notes that you have for sale.
Produce a report that:

- shows only the records that fulfil these criteria;

- shows only the fields *Denomination, PickNo, Serial, Cashier, Condition, Value* with labels and data fully visible;

- sorts records into decreasing order of *Value*;

- fits to a single portrait page;

- calculates the total sale price of all the listed banknotes, with a suitable label, placed as the last line of the report;

- has a heading **Listing for C Boyd**;

- has your name, today's date and your email address in the report header. [7 marks]

8 **Evidence 3**. Take screenshot of the query used to produce this report and insert it into your evidence document. [1 mark]

9 Save and print the report. [1 mark]

10 You are summarising the information in *BanknoteSale*.
Produce a query which, for each *Cashier*, counts the number of banknotes for sale and the total *Value* of those banknotes. [3 marks]

Save the results in a format that can be used in a word processed document.

11 **Evidence 4**. Import the results saved in step 10 to your evidence document. [1 mark]

Total marks available: 30. To check your work, download the completed version of **BanknoteTradeFair.pdf**, **BanknoteBoyd.pdf** and the evidence document **EvidencePracticalDatabase.pdf**.

Web authoring (1)

Webpages can be created in a number of ways:

- use a basic text editor to write **HTML**;
- use WYSIWIG software such as Microsoft's Expression Web, Adobe's Dreamweaver or open source alternatives such as BlueGriffon;
- use an online content management system (CMS).

There are three web development layers:

- Content layer: the actual content of the webpages. Created using HTML (HyperText Mark-up Language).
- Presentation layer: information specifying the appearance of the webpage content. Applied through a cascading style sheet (extension .css).
- Behaviour layer: real-time interactive content that is added to a webpage.

Tables

The basic structure of many webpages is built around, or includes, one or more tables. This allows information on the page to be laid out very easily. Even though the grid lines (borders) of the table are not usually visible, if you look carefully at how the information on a page appears, it will be apparent that a table is behind the design.

Parrot	Population
Cape	1200
Echo Parakeet	700
Lilian's Lovebird	15000
Seychelles Parrot	650
Africa species	26

Table header

Table body
– 4 rows
– 8 cells of table data

Table footer

A table has various elements, all of which can have individual styles applied to them – either inline or through a style sheet (see below). Make sure you know the html tags that identify them. Inline styles mean that the specified style applies to that particular element at that time.

The opening lines of the html for this table could be:

```
<table style="width: 20%" border="0">
    <tr align="center">
        <td bgcolor="#009900"><font face ="Calibri" color="#CC0000">Parrot</font></td>
        <td bgcolor="#009900"><font face ="Calibri" color="#CC0000">Population</font></td>
    </tr>
    <tr>
        <td align="center">Cape</td>
        <td align="right">1200</td>
    </tr>
```

producing:

Parrot	Population
Cape	1200
Echo Parakeet	700

These inline instructions regarding style, although immediate and easily added, are not efficient. If the same styles were to be applied to every data cell they need adding into every <td> definition of the table. Also, if the text colour needed changing, the same change will need applying to every instance of its use. For this reason, style sheets are created and applied.

A cell in a table can hold a variety of objects such as: text, pictures, video clips or sound. Adding a photo into the cell requires a reference to be made to where the photo is stored. Placing an image of an Echo Parakeet into the 3rd row of the table instead of the text could be achieved by adding the tag:

<img src="Echo_Parakeet" align="middle" height="100" width="75" alt="Echo Parakeet"/>

Make sure you understand the effect of each of the parts of this tag.

Lists of data items <li> can be ordered <ol> or unordered <ul>. Ordered lists have each list item preceded by a number (1, 2, 3, ...) or a letter (a, b, c, ...) of various styles. Unordered lists have a bullet point preceding each list item, which can be specified.

This list could be produced by:

1. Cockatiel
2. African Grey Parrot
3. Budgerigars
4. Cockatoos
5. Conures

```
<ol>
  <li>Cockatiel</li>
  <li>African Grey Parrot</li>
  <li>Budgerigars</li>
  <li>Cockatoos</li>
  <li>Conures</li>
</ol>
```

Style sheets

A **style sheet** holds all the definitions or declarations of the styles that are to be applied – usually across the whole of a website. The .css file to be used is referenced in the <head> section of webpage's HTML.

Styles that may need their declarations creating or adjusting are:

CSS style	Purpose	What might need to be adjusted
body	Starts the HTML section for the actual content of the webpage	A background colour or image
table, tr, th, td	Often used to structure the content of a web page as well as display particular information within a webpage	A table's overall size, merging columns or rows, column width and row height, make the row/column headings appear differently to the table's data, the thickness/visibility of the table gridlines, the 'space' between cells and around the data in a cell
h1, h2, h3, h4, h5, h6, p	Headings and paragraph styles	A particular or default font typeface, its size, colour, alignment, style
ol, ul, li	Creation of lists that are either numbered (ordered) or bulleted (unordered)	A list's style, including a particular style of bullet point for an unordered list

All style definitions start with a keyword followed by the definition inside a pair of { }. The definition is made up of a number of properties with that property's value followed by a ;.

Example 1

p {font-family: "Britannic Bold"; color: #B0560C; font-style: italic; font-size: 50pt; text-align: center;}

… results in paragraph text displayed as **Britannic Bold**, brown, italicised, large size, centred in the line.

Note:

- the font style has quotation marks around it because it is more than a single word;
- the American spellings of *color* and *center*;
- the colour is written in **hexadecimal**, B0 is the 'amount' of red, 56 of green, 0C of blue. 00 would be zero of that colour and FF is the full amount of that colour. Start with a #.

Example 2

table {width: 75 per cent; border: 5px solid #0000FF; border-spacing: 5px;}
td {border: 2px solid #000000; padding: 20px;}

… results in a table with these characteristics:

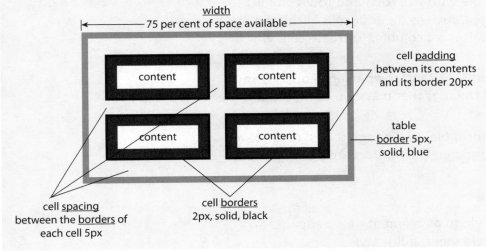

width
75 per cent of space available

cell padding
between its contents
and its border 20px

table
border 5px,
solid, blue

cell spacing
between the borders of
each cell 5px

cell borders
2px, solid, black

 Revision tip

It is essential to check each style definition for correct syntax. A misplaced or missing ;, { or } can completely change the effectiveness of the style sheet by invalidating one or more definitions.

 Revision tip

In hexadecimal, #FFFFFF is white (all colour mixed in) and #000000 is black (absence of any colour).

 Revision tip

Draw and annotate a table design in rough, like the diagram here, including all the features that are needed, before typing up the definitions.

 Revision tip

Keep all files – html, css, images – in the same folder.

Quick test

Are the following statements true or false?

A cascading style sheet is referenced in the <body> section of a webpage.	
An unordered list, ul, can have the type of bullet image defined.	
#FA3G0 is a valid hexadecimal value to define a colour.	
h1 {font-family: Times New Roman; colour: #FFCC00;} is a valid declaration.	
Styles consist of properties and their values.	
The text that appears in a web page is within the content layer of the page.	

Web authoring (2)

From the webpage http://www.collins.co.uk/IGCSEICTrevision download these files into a new folder in your workspace: **ppshome.txt**, **ppsstyles.txt**, **banner2.jpg**, **PatagonianConure.jpg**, **PinkCockatoo.jpg**, **BlueGoldMacaw.jpg**.

The structure of a webpage

A webpage can be considered as a table with some cells being merged to form complete rows or columns.

Look at the html coding for this simple table and make the connections between the order of the tags and the appearance of the table cells.

Open **ppshome.txt** and **ppsstyles.txt** in your web authoring software. Save **ppshome** as a webpage (extensions of **.html** or **.htm** for example) and **ppsstyles** as a cascading style sheet, CSS (extension of **.css**). Open ppshome.html in a web browser and you should see a webpage for Pete's Parrot Sanctuary with a blue background and three images.

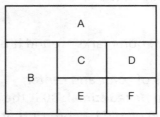

```
<table>
    <tr>
        <td colspan=3> A </td>
    </tr>
    <tr>
        <td rowspan=2> B </td>
        <td> C </td>
        <td> D </td>
    </tr>
    <tr>
        <td> E </td>
        <td> F </td>
    </tr>
</table>
```

Now look at the Pete's Parrot Sanctuary webpage. You should be able to see that the page is based on a table with five rows and four columns. Some of the cells have been merged, such as the four cells in the top row and the three middle cells in the left-most column, to create cells which span multiple rows and columns.

In the html coding for *ppshome* find the tags: rowpan and colspan, and make the connection between all the tags that make up the table and the appearance of the webpage.

Look at the stylesheet definition for *table, td*. Change the '3' to '0', save the style sheet and refresh the webpage. The borders are not displayed, making the webpage cleaner.

Applying styles to a webpage

There are three ways to apply a style to an element of a webpage: an external style sheet, an internal style sheet, inline styles.

For an external stylesheet, in the <head> section of *ppshome* is the instruction:

> **<link rel="stylesheet" type="text/css" href="ppsstyles.css"/>**

will bring into the webpage all the styles declared in the file *ppsstyle.css*.

These three methods for applying styles have hierarchical precedence and unless fully understood, mixing them up may have unexpected outcomes. A good general rule is to remember that the last style applied before it is used is the one that takes effect.

Attaching an external stylesheet is the preferred and most effective method of applying styles across a website. The styles are held in one document, the stylesheet, and by attaching the link to the stylesheet into the <head> section of each webpage the styles are uniformly applied to

> **Revision tip**
>
> Read through *ppsstyles.ccs* and make sure that you note ideas such as grouping together properties that are common to a number of elements such as font colour for H1, H2 and H3.

every webpage in the website. The styles as written in the stylesheet could be inserted into the <head> section of a webpage – an internal stylesheet. These will take effect only over this webpage, although they could be copied into other <head> sections of other webpages. However, if a style needed changing, it would need changing on every webpage that style has been added to. Inline styles are mentioned above, and once again any change will need to be made for every instance of that style in the webpage.

If a style is defined more than once, for example h1 is defined in an attached external stylesheet and then again as an individual style in the <head> section, the one that is encountered last is the one that will be applied. So, if in the <body> section h1 has another style applied, then that will be the latest, and used, definition.

For example, this stylesheet:

```
<style>
table{width: 20%; border: 0p}
th{background-color:#009900}
td{font-family: calibri; font-size:20px; text-align: center}
h1{font-family: "chiller"; font-size:25px; text-align: center}
</style>

</head>

<body>

<table>
    <thead>
    <tr>
        <th><h1>Parrot</h1></td>
        <th><h1><font face="broadway">Population</font></h1></td>
    </tr>
    </thead>
    <tr>
        <td>Cape</td>
        <td>1200</td>
    </tr>
    <tr>
        <td><font face="Times New Roman">Echo Parakeet</font></td>
        <td>700</td>
    </tr>
```

produces the effects:

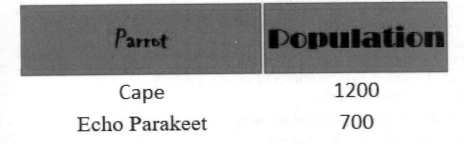

Notice that the style for the text 'Population' has been overwritten in font Broadway because that is the latest definition to be applied to that element. In the same way, the text 'Echo Parakeet' is displayed in 'Times New Roman' instead of Calibri, again because it was the last style to be defined for that text.

Hyperlinks and anchors

There are three hyperlinks in the left-most column of *ppshome.html*, attached to *Ask the experts*, *Licences* and *World Parrot Trust*:

<a href="http://worldparrottrust.org">World Parrot Trust</a> takes you to the website of the World Parrot Trust. The website will open in the current window.

<a href="licences.html" target="_licence">Licences</a> will open a webpage (*licences.html*), located in the same directory as *ppshome.html*, in a new window (referenced as *_licence*). (Note: you do not have this page.)

<a href="mailto:expert@petesparrots.org?subject=Question">Ask the Experts</a> launches your default email application and opens a new message addressed to *expert@petesparrots.org* with *Question* as the subject of the email.

There is one anchor – at the bottom of the table. Clicking on this takes you back to a bookmark at the top of the page – useful if the webpage is particularly long.

Anchors and hyperlinks redirect the user to new locations. An anchor is a specific link within a webpage which is useful in long pages with lots of content. Because anchors are locations on a webpage rather than an object you do not see them when the page is viewed with a browser. Hyperlinks are created on objects in the webpage such as text or images. Clicking on them redirects you to another location away from the current webpage. The three examples above are connected to text within the webpage. The first one takes you to another website completely (worldparrottrust.org) and the second one redirects to another webpage within the current website (licences.html). The third one opens up the default email application as described.

Testing and publishing a website

It is difficult to edit a webpage after it has been uploaded to the internet so thorough testing beforehand is essential. It is not enough to ask, 'Does the site work?' You need to consider, among other things, the text (check for spelling, grammar, font choice), images and other media (clarity, suitability, size, playing of media content), hyperlinks (internal, external, anchors), consistency (use of css files), and browser compatibility (effectiveness in different browsers, including mobile devices).

You need to create a test plan which considers what might and should actually happen when users access the website. The test plan will contain a list of tests to be carried out (does a particular image hyperlink take the user to the desired resource, file or webpage?), how that test is to be tested (click on the link), what the expected result should be (directed to the correct resource), and any action required if the test fails.

In order for a wider audience to access a website on the internet it needs to be published (uploaded) to a web server. A web hosting company will provide storage space on their servers that are directly connected to the internet. The most common method for transferring files from your computer system to the host company is to use File Transfer Protocol (FTP), which provides controlled access to your specific file space on the web server. An FTP utility allows you to see the file structure on the web server, just as you do on your own computer, and then to drag and drop files in the server file folders.

If you have had difficulty with your web authoring software, download **PeteParrotWebpage.pdf**.

> **Revision tip**

Make sure you know the syntax and effects of hyperlinks and anchors.

Quick test

Are the following statements true or false?

The *Mailto* element of a hyperlink is used to send an instant message.	
A style sheet is recognised by the extension .css.	
rowspan enables a cell's content to be displayed in many rows.	
<table> contains *<row>* which contains *<td>*.	
Style definitions can be grouped together.	
A webpage based on a table must have an equal number of rows and columns.	

Exam-style practice questions

You are going to produce a webpage for inclusion in an existing website.

From http://www.collins.co.uk/IGCSEICTrevision you will need to download the following: **cbestyles. txt, Banner.jpg, ChiefCashiers.txt, PeppiattBrown10Shilling.jpg, HollomBrown10Shilling.jpg, PeppiattMauve10Shilling.jpg, cbeB235.txt.**

1 Open **cbestyles.txt** in your web authoring software and then save it as a cascading style sheet with the name **cbestyles.css**.

2 In your web authoring software create a new webpage called **cbe10shillings.html**.
Create a structure, using a table, that will look like this:

A	
B	
C	D
E	F
	G
	H
I	J

The table is 1200px wide and centred in the browser.
Row B is 75px high.
Row C and the last row are 50px high.
Cells C, E and I are 300px wide.   [9 marks]

3 Place the image **Banner.jpg** in cell A.   [1 mark]

4 In cell B insert the text: **Ten Shillings**.   [1 mark]

5 In cell C type in: **You are at: Home, Ten Shillings**.   [1 mark]

6 In cell D type in: **Click on a banknote image to view its details**.   [1 mark]

7 In cell I type in: **Return to top**.   [1 mark]

8 In cell J type in your name and today's date.   [1 mark]

9 Apply the paragraph style to text in cells C, D, I and J.
Apply the h1 style to the text in cell B.   [1 mark]

10 The text for cell E is in **ChiefCashiers.txt**. Apply style h2 to this text and make the list of seven names an unordered list.   [2 marks]

11 In cell F place the image **PeppiattBrown10Shilling.jpg**.   [1 mark]

12 Resize the image **HollomBrown10Shilling.jpg** to have a width of 600px maintaining aspect ratio and place in cell G.   [2 marks]

13 In cell H place the image **PeppiattMauve10Shilling.jpg**.   [1 mark]

14 Add a hyperlink to the word **Home** in cell C to open the webpage **cbehome.html**. The webpage is to open in the current window. (Note: you do not have this webpage.) [3 marks]

15 Add a hyperlink to the image in cell F to open the webpage **cbeB235.html** in a new window called **_B235**. [3 marks]

16 In cell B place an anchor with the id **Top**. Add a hyperlink to the text **top** in cell I to take you to the anchor in cell B. [2 marks]

17 The style sheet has some mistakes in it. The company style guide has these entries:

- background colour for a webpage should be the mix: Green #00, Blue #99, Red #00;

- text colour for h1, h2, h3 and li should be the mix: Blue #99, Red #cc, Green #ff;

- cell borders for tables should have a thickness of 0px and be collapsed;

- paragraph text should be white and centred in its cell. [4 marks]

Correct the mistakes in the style sheet and save it as **cbestyles02.css**. [1 mark]

Attach this style sheet to your webpage. [1 mark]

18 Save your webpage.

19 In your web authoring software open **cbeB235.txt** and save it as a webpage called **cbeB235.html**.

20 Attach the stylesheet **cbestyles02.css** to this webpage. [1 mark]

21 In the bottom row of the table add a hyperlink to the word **here**. The hyperlink will launch the user's default email application and open a new message addressed to **colin@colinsbanknoteemporium.net** with the subject **Bid for B235**. [3 marks]

22 Apply style h1 to **Peppiatt 10/– note**. Apply style h2 to the other details in the right-hand cell. Apply the paragraph style to the text in the bottom row. [3 marks]

23 Save the webpage.

24 Print browser views of **cbe10shillings.html** and of **cbeB235.html**. [2 marks]

25 Print the HTML code for **cbe10shillings.html** and of **cbeB235.html**.

26 Print a copy of **cbestyle02.css**. The solutions: browser printouts, HTML coding and the style sheet details, can be downloaded from the webpage, **cbeBanknote.pdf**.

Total marks available: 45.

Glossary

Actuator

A device which takes a signal from a computer and converts it into motion or controlled movement, for example, switching a heater on or off, controlling a motor.

Analogue data

Data that can take any value on a scale, varying continuously.

Analogue to digital convertor (ADC)

A device that converts analogue signals like those produced by a sensor to a digital signal a computer can process.

Applications software

Software that will carry out specific tasks on a computer such as word processing or using a database.

Artificial intelligence biometrics

Coupling the latest advances in biometrics with artificial intelligence to create systems that will recognise individuals based on, e.g. fingerprint or facial recognition.

ATM (automated teller machine)

Remotely connected to a bank's computer system, it can dispense cash and provide account information.

Backing storage

Devices that allow large amounts of data to be stored outside the main or central memory, e.g. CD, DVD, memory stick.

Backup

An extra copy of computer information that can be used if the original copy is damaged or corrupted.

Basic Input and Output System (BIOS)

Start-up code that enables the operating system to be loaded and the computer to start successfully.

Bluetooth

A radio technology that allows signals to be transmitted wirelessly over short distances between telephones, computers and devices.

Central processing unit (CPU)

The part of a computer that controls all the other parts. Designs vary but, generally, the CPU consists of the control unit, the arithmetic and logic unit and memory.

Command Line Interface (CLI)

The type of user interface where the user needs to type in a single line of text that is a direct command to the operating system.

Cryptography

Protecting information by transforming it (encrypting) into something that is unreadable unless you know how it has been scrambled.

Cyberbullying

Using technology to bully people. It can include texting, instant messaging, and posting on social media and gaming websites.

Desktop computer

A general purpose computer made up of: monitor, keyboard, mouse, processor and storage.

Desktop publishing

Application software that allows text and graphics to be combined to produce professional looking material for publication, e.g. newsletters, flyers.

Digital data

Data that has binary representation. Information is represented as a series of 0s and 1s.

Digital to analogue convertor (DAC)

A device that converts digital signals produced by a processor into an analogue signal to control a device via an actuator.

Direct entry devices

A device that can transfer data automatically from source to the processor, such as a barcode reader.

Drop-down list

A graphical user interface control that allows the user to choose an item from a list.

Electronic Funds transfer (EFT)

The process of transferring currency electronically between two banks.

Electronic Funds Transfer POS (EFTPOS)

The ability to pay for goods and services electronically, allowing direct computer access between banks and service providers.

Electronic Point Of Sale (EPOS)

Using technology for the efficient recording of the sale of goods or services to a customer by scanning barcodes, retrieving information and updating data files.

Encryption

The process of scrambling a piece of information so that it can only be read by the owner of the encryption key.

E-safety

The safe and responsible use of technology. This includes the use of the internet and other means of communication using electronic media (e.g. text messages, gaming devices, email, etc).

Facial recognition systems

A type of biometric software application that can identify a specific individual in a digital image by comparing selected facial features in the image with a facial database.

Field

A single item of data, such as a name, account number or stock level.

File

A collection of data or instructions; a program, an image, a database, a document.

Filter

The set of criteria that is applied to a dataset.

Flat file database

A single collection of structured data.

Footer

A 'reserved' area at the foot of a document between the bottom edge and the margin of the page.

Foreign key

A field within a record that contains the primary key to a record in another table, creating a relationship between the two tables.

Graphical User Interface (GUI)

The type of user interface where the user controls the operation of the computer by using a pointing device to select icons on screen.

Hacking

Gaining unauthorised access to a computer system.

Hardware

The physical components of a computer system, e.g. mouse, monitor, printer.

Header

A 'reserved' area at the top of a document between the top edge and margin of the page.

Hexadecimal (hex)

A counting system that uses 16 characters and simplifies how binary is represented. A hex digit can be any of the following 16 digits: **0 1 2 3 4 5 6 7 8 9 A B C D E F.**

Holography

A technique that uses photographic projection to create a three-dimensional image.

HTML

HyperText Mark-up Language, a coding language developed to design the layout of webpages.

Human–computer interface (HCI)

Any software or hardware that allows a user to interact with a computer, for example, GUI, HCI or virtual reality.

Hyperlinks

A piece of text, image or graphic that when clicked takes the user to a specified webpage, resource or website.

Icon

A small graphic or logo representing a piece of software, a particular command or function, or a brand.

Input devices

Items of hardware that are a means of entering data into a computer.

Internet

A wide area network (WAN). A global network which allows anyone connected to it to access information located anywhere else across the network, provided they have permission. Sometimes referred to as a network of networks.

Internet Service Provider (ISP)

A company that provides users access to the internet, usually for a regular fee.

Intranet

A local area network that allows the sharing of files and the sending of messages between users but without access to the internet.

Laptop/notebook computer

A small portable computer where all the components are together in a single compact unit.

Main memory

Memory chip(s) physically located very close to the processor which holds programs of data that the processor needs immediately.

Mainframe

A physically large computer with very fast processor speeds and large memory capacity that is capable of complex problem-solving using very large amounts of data.

Microprocessor

A special kind of CPU used in PCs, smaller computers and small computerised devices such as washing machines.

Modem

A device used to connect to the internet via the telephone line. It is both an ADC and a DAC since the telephone line requires an analogue signal.

Motherboard

The main circuit board of the computer and is also known as the mainboard or logic board, holding all the vital electronic system components.

Multimedia presentations
Combining sound, images, video and animation to present information.

Network Interface Card (NIC)
A hardware device required in any computer wishing to connect to a network.

Networked computers
When a set of computers are linked together to allow sharing resources such as files, printers, an internet connection.

Open source
A type of software that is freely available, whose users are encouraged to suggest or submit modifications and developments that become incorporated into the software.

Operating system
A systems software program that controls the entire operation of the computer as well as allowing interaction with the user. Popular operating systems include Windows, Apple OS and Linux.

Option group
A graphical user interface control that allows the user to select between usually two options. Often uses radio buttons to achieve this.

Output devices
Items of hardware that allow the results of processing to be presented to the user (or to another device).

Password
A personal identification phrase or collection of characters that in conjunction with a user's ID will allow access to a system.

Peripheral
Any piece of hardware connected to a computer, outside the CPU and working memory.

Pharming
A scamming practice where users are redirected to a fake version of a website in order to collect personal/security information from the user, who believes they are at the genuine site. This occurs because their server has been infected by malware.

Phishing
A scamming practice where users receive an email that looks as if it comes from a genuine organisation, but when the user clicks on a link they are directed to a fake website.

Primary key
A field in a record that contains a unique data value and is used to identify that record.

Proxy server
A server that allows multiple computers to connect to the internet but can filter their access and cache pages for quick access.

Query
A search request with specific criteria applied to a database table that returns a subset of the dataset.

Random Access Memory (RAM)
An internal memory chip that holds data temporarily while applications are running.

Read Only Memory (ROM)
An internal memory chip that stores data or instructions that need to be permanent, such as BIOS.

Record
A collection of related fields. A set of information about one item that the file is about, such as a book, a car, a student.

Record structure
The collection of fields and their properties such as data type or size, which make up a record.

Relational database
A database that has links (relationships) with data held in different tables.

Repetitive Strain Injury (RSI)
Aching muscular injury occurring from carrying out an action such as texting or using a mouse continuously over a long time period.

Robotics
The use of computer-controlled machinery to perform manual tasks. This has been especially successful on assembly lines in the manufacturing industries.

Router
A device that connects different networks together. This may be two LANs or a home computer and the internet.

Run-time created field
A field that is added to a report (or query) which displays a value calculated as the report (or query result) is being compiled.

Smishing
The scam of phishing but applied to mobile phones, with users being sent SMS messages asking them log in to a fake website.

Software
The programs, instructions and data that enable the computer to carry out a task.

Spam
The use of email systems to send large qualities of unwanted advertisements for goods and services to multiple addresses at once. Often linked to criminal business methods, computer viruses and identity theft.

Spyware
Software that is installed on a user's computer without their knowledge. It collects browsing habits/information that has been typed in and then transmits it to the originator of the software.

Stand-alone computers
Computers that are not connected to a network and are used as an isolated work station; they do not share any resources such as files, storage or printers.

Storage device
A device into which data can be placed, held and later retrieved from.

Style sheet
A collection of styles that is to be applied across a range of pages in a website. The style sheet is saved as a separate file in a .css format.

System software
The name given to software such as operating systems and utility programs that control and maintain the computer system.

Tablet computer
A small, wireless, portable computer with a touch-screen interface.

Teleworking
A working pattern that allows people to use ICT technology to enable them to work from home rather than travelling to an office.

Text translation
Software that combines dictionaries, parallel texts, translation memory and language search engines to break a text into small segments, which are then compared with previously saved translated segments.

User ID
A personal identification term that allows access to a system such as an email address or 'nickname', usually in conjunction with a password.

User interface
The way in which the user and the computer interact. The design of this interface is important as it affects, for example, how users input data, or how the software presents information to the user.

Validation
A software check to ensure that the data that has been entered can be used by the system. It is a check to see that the data entered lies within specified limits or fits a particular format.

Verification
A manual check for transcription errors during data entry – checking accuracy after entering or copying data. There are two methods of verification: visual check; double entry.

Video conferencing
Using webcams or video cameras and computers, usually linked together by the internet, to carry out a real-time conversation across any distance.

Virtual reality
An artificial environment that is created with software and presented to the user in such a way that the user accepts it as a real environment. This is primarily experienced through sight and sound, with the user wearing a special headset. Recent developments include body suits that give more stimulus than just sight and sound.

Vishing
The voicemail equivalent of smishing.

Vision enhancement
Devices that enable images to be formed by intensifying or enhancing the low level of existing light – most commonly recognised as night-vision scopes. Also images can be enhanced by capturing infrared light and producing a thermal image.

Voice Over Internet Protocol (VOIP)
Instead of using the normal telephone network (designed to carry voices using analogue signals), VOIP systems route voice conversations through the internet as digital data, just like any other internet data, meaning the conversation is, essentially, free.

Web authoring
Application software that allows the user to create, edit and format web pages.

WiFi
A system allowing computers to connect to networks using wireless communication.

WIMP systems
Windows, Icons, Menu, Pointing device. A type of GUI.

Word processing
Application software that allows the user to create, edit and format documents.

Answers

All exam-style questions, related example answers given on the website, marks awarded and comments that appear in this book were written by the author. In examinations, the way marks are awarded to questions and answers like these may be different.

		Marks
Chapter 1. Types and components of computer systems		
p. 10	Quick test: T, T, F, F, T, T	
p. 12	Quick test: T, F, F, F, T, F	
p. 14	Quick test: F, F, T, F, T, F	
Exam-style practice questions		
1.	**Hardware**: Disk drive, RAM chip. **Software**: Spreadsheet, File manager, Windows 8/Android.	3
2.	**Application**: Web browser, Database. **System**: File conversion program, File compression program, BIOS.	3
3.	**Peripherals**: Mouse, Scanner, Printer.	3
4.	Files are accessible from any location across a range of devices, but security and cost of the storage area could be concerns.	2
5.	RAM stores data temporarily, but ROM is fixed at manufacture. RAM can hold GBs of information but ROM has quite a small capacity.	2
6.	Tablets and smartphones are both portable and have touch-sensitive screens.	2
7.	They enable files to become portable, provide cheap storage and are durable.	2
8.	A laptop has a built-in hard drive so that data that is collected can be stored. Any application that the salesman needs to run will have more functionality than would be available as an app for a tablet.	2
9.	The microprocessor cannot be re-programmed to do anything other than the task that it is designed for. It can be 'programmed' to follow certain wash cycles – part of its functionality.	2
10.	Networked computers can share files and devices but a stand-alone computer is not connected to any other computers and so files cannot be shared. Office computers are usually networked and single home computers are often stand-alone devices.	1 2
11.	Mainframe computers work at very high speeds and can access and process vast amounts of data. A network of desktop computers would not have the processing capacity or speed that the bank requires, where hundreds of thousands of transactions a day will be processed. There will also be a vast requirement for data storage.	4
12.	A GUI is operated by clicking or touching icons on a screen. This is a very simple way to operate a computer and make apps work. A CLI needs specialised instructions to be typed in. For children to effectively operate a device, tapping on an icon will be far more successful (and enjoyable).	3
13.	A ROM chip is a read only device. Any information stored on it is placed there at manufacture. It is not possible for Jonas to have stored anything on a ROM chip.	2
14.	Fingerprint technology could be used in the dining hall to identify students and, once their food bill has been created, debit the amount from their stored credit, making it a cashless environment. Registrations (and movement around school) could be tracked using an RFID system with tags on badges or ID cards on lanyard straps.	4
Chapter 2. Input and output devices		
p. 19	Quick test: F, F, T, F, T, F	
p. 20	Quick test: F, F, T, T, F, F	
Exam-style practice questions		
1.	**Input**: oxygen level sensor, TV remote control, data gloves. **Output**: heater, thermal printer.	3
2.	Some input devices such as a sensor collect data that is analogue. This needs to be converted into binary form so that the processor can use it.	1

		Marks
3.	A dot matrix printer is an impact printer, which prints character by character in the same way a typewriter works, and cannot print graphics. A laser printer works in a similar way to a photocopier, using toner, and can print high-quality photographic images.	2
4.	Optical Mark Reader.	1
5.	**Input**: bar code reader, keyboard, touch screen. **Output**: printer, screen, loudspeaker.	3
6.	Sound waves are analogue data and the computer produces a digital output signal.	1
7.	Iris recognition: airline check-in/passport control. Fingerprint recognition: access to an examination room.	2
8.	**Input**: moisture sensor (with ADC). **Output**: actuator to control valves on the sprinklers.	2
9.	Voice recognition systems can identify particular people and allow them to give commands. Advantages: enhanced security, may enable a disabled driver to effectively control a car, driver is not required to physically operate a device (entertainment system). Disadvantages: background noise (radio, conversations) might interfere with accuracy of command recognition, certain words used as commands may occur in conversation.	4
10.	Farmer can track movement of animals and it enables accurate record-keeping, for example of vaccinations. Tags on animals quickly implemented, effective recording of movement between fields/pens/vehicles, but could be a costly initial set-up and cost-ineffective if only a small number of animals.	3

Chapter 3. Storage devices and media, ICT in banking

p. 23	Quick test: F, F, T, T, T, F	
p. 24	Quick test: F, T, F, F, T, F	

Exam-style practice questions

1.	**Magnetic**: cassette tape, removable hard disk drive. **Optical**: CD/DVD, Blu-ray. **Solid state**: memory stick.	3
2.	Magnetic tape.	1
3.	A CD is a write only once disk, such as a music CD, which means he cannot amend the information on it, he'd need to save on a new one. He should have used a CD-RW, a DVD-RW or a high capacity memory stick.	3
4.	**Advantages**: saves on property rental, money saved can be invested in call-centres, online banking technology or larger centralised bank branches. **Disadvantages**: customers lose contact with someone with local knowledge, customers face a longer journey to talk to someone or to conduct business (for instance setting up a mortgage), customers are forced to use telebanking or online banking, which they may be reluctant (or unable) to use.	2, 2
5.	Files are stored on a remote data server. **Advantages**: files can be accessed/shared by many people, from any location, over a range of devices. **Disadvantage**: currently the biggest concern is security, but cost may also be a factor.	1, 2

Chapter 4. Computer networks and the effects of using them

p. 28	Quick test: F, T, T, T, F, F	
p. 30	Quick test: T, F, T, F, F, T	
p. 32	Quick test: T, F, T, T, F, F	
p. 34	Quick test: F, T, F, T, F, F	
p. 37	Quick test: F, F, T, T, F T	

Exam-style practice questions

1.	Needed: bridge, switch, modem.	3
2.	True: A LAN connects computers over a small area; WANs enable very fast data transfer between multinational organisations.	2
3.	True: A booking system has to work in real time; The LAN in a doctor's surgery will probably be connected to a local hospital network.	2

		Marks
4.	Advantage: data can be shared between the LAN users. Disadvantage: security/integrity of data is compromised.	2
5.	Wireless access point, boosters (amplifiers).	2
6.	Transfer of files directly between two computers across the internet.	1
7.	The mechanic responds to a variety of questions. The inference engine uses the rules base to match answers to data stored in the system's knowledge base, refining questions and narrowing down the likely problem. The system then suggests how the problem can be fixed.	3
8.	Advantage: access to company data and applications is more flexible with a WLAN. Disadvantage: employees can be anywhere across the site, but the company network managers need to ensure that access to the WLAN is strongly protected.	2
9.	Quicker and cheaper to build a model than the real bridge. Stress testing safer using the model than the real bridge.	2
10.	The intranet does not have a connection to the internet so to allow this a router is needed. Advantage: access to the internet will allow customers to order via the new company website. Disadvantage: opening up their system to the internet brings security problems: hacking, virus infection.	1, 1, 2
11.	This keeps all communication within the confines of the application, over which the organisation has a degree of control. It means that users are not vulnerable to email scams such as phishing and spam.	2
12.	A website is generally used to promote a company, not provide a front for simply downloading files, and any file would need to be securely protected. The company might also choose to store data in the cloud, but transferring files between their various facilities using FTP is quick, secure and effective, keeping data files within the company.	2
Chapter 5. The effects of using ICT		
p. 41	Quick test: T, F, F, F, T, T	
p. 43	Quick test: T, T, F, F, F, T	
p. 45	Quick test: T, F, F, T, T, F	
Exam-style practice questions		
1.	Advantages: Better monitoring of stock levels; Less cash handled at the checkout; Fewer staff required at checkouts.	3
2.	True: Copyright law exists to protect the income of resource creators; A washing machine is a microprocessor-controlled device; Contactless payments can be made at EFTPOS terminals.	3
3.	Any three from: microwave oven, washing machine, dishwasher, refrigerator, oven.	3
4.	Trailing wires/cables (tie them safely together, lay them under matting, use wireless connection), electrocution from spilt drinks or exposed wires (do not allow food or drink near computers, ensure plugs are wired correctly/safely).	2
5.	Physical: use of distinctive holograms on packaging. Software: online registration to receive an activation code.	2
6.	Giving a multimedia presentation in another part of the building, checking/updating stock levels in storerooms, working with distant colleagues via a conference call.	2
7.	Retraining involves learning new skills for a new job; deskilling means that a job now requires a lower level of skill than previously needed.	2
8.	Inputs: sensors for temperature and oxygen levels, keypad/screen to input the required temperature and oxygen level. Processing: comparison of required levels against the actual levels, instruction to switch on/off the heater or pump. Outputs: heater to warm the water, pump to introduce oxygen, screen to display temperature and oxygen levels, an actuator to switch the heater/pump on/off.	6
9.	A controlled internet would help with: prevention of illegal material posted on internet; guarantee of content accuracy. Creating an organisation to control the internet would present many difficulties: who pays for it? Would that mean the internet ceases to be free? Who agrees the standards (cultural, political, religious)? Material that is illegal, despite its availability online, is already covered by various laws.	3

		Marks
10.	Information in a database can be related, meaning that search results can include related or recommended resources as well as resources strictly matching the search criteria; the information can be accessed by more than one person at a time; if linked to borrowing information it can indicate more reliably that a resource is currently available/unavailable.	2
11.	Advantages: the company will need fewer people in the warehouse; the robots can collect products without needing a rest break; collection of products will be quick and accurate. Disadvantages: the company needs employees to program and maintain the robots; requires large investment in technology, Work change: employees are needed only to pack and not to collect; employees' work will be less strenuous.	3,2

Chapter 6. Data types and databases

p. 50	Quick test: F, T, T, F, F, T	
p. 52	Quick test: F, T, F, T, F, T	

Exam-style practice questions

1.	a) text b) key field c) OLE d) Boolean.	4
2.	Sort: To list all the winners by the year of the tournaments. Search: To find details about a particular winner.	2
3.	To be able to make special offers to loyal customers based on their shopping habits; to analyse sales in the shop based on loyal customer demographics (age, gender …).	2
4.	ABD 439, DZH 236, BZE 439, ALZ 128, JFA 857, AVN 192, AHG 243, CCA 876.	3

Chapter 7. Systems analysis and design

p. 56	Quick test: F, T, F, T, F, F	
p. 60	Quick test: F, T, F, T, T, F	

Exam-style practice questions

1.	Verification: ensuring that data input is the data that was intended. Validation: ensuring that the data that is entered can be used by the system. Verification is a manual process but validation is a software process.	2, 1
2.	(table below)	3, 2, 2, 2

Data item	Normal	Extreme	Abnormal
Licence plate	COL 1N	A	CPS 1000R
Components changed	4	99	Ten
Hours worked	6	8	9

3.	Technical: hardware and software requirements; file (table) structures and a list of field names; systems flowcharts/algorithms and program listings. User: installation guide; error handling/FAQ.	3, 2
4.	Direct changeover. Benefits will be seen immediately, low cost, no reorganisation needed, minimal training.	1, 2
5.	Interview the three supervisors because they will have an overview of the whole system. With there only being three of them this will not be a lengthy process. They will also have good ideas of the strengths and weaknesses of the current system together with, perhaps, realistic ideas of development. Create questionnaires for the remainder of the workforce in order to collect information about the general day-to-day running of the current system. They may be able to help identify the strengths and weaknesses from the viewpoint of their role in the current system. You may only get this one opportunity to collect information so it is important that the questionnaire is designed to get as much relevant information as possible. Observing the system in operation is an excellent way to get a feel for the way the system works: who deals with which items of data, what is done with data in terms of storage and processing as well as receiving and giving information. Sometimes it is useful to shadow an employee for a day or even follow a piece of paper (an order, or delivery note) through the system.	6

		Marks
Chapter 8. Safety and security		
p. 63	Quick test: T, T, F, F, F, T	
p. 65	Quick test: T, F, F, F, T, T	
Exam-style practice questions		
1.	OK: first name; favourite meal; pet's name (possibly – many people use things like this for passwords).	3
2.	Identity theft: reveal as little about yourself as possible; it's a make-believe world so create an imaginary/fantasy you. Credit card fraud: refuse to buy in-game extras. These games can also become addictive or you may be bullied into being online 'with your team/friends/tribe …' so put limits on your time in the game.	4
3.	Phishing: an attempt to get a user to provide personal/security details by sending an email purporting to come from, for example, their bank, asking for a reply which should contain certain details. Pharming may also start with an email but users are directed to a fake website where personal/security details need to be typed in.	1
4.	Social networking sites have millions of members and most people are all too happy to make a friend connection when requested, even though the request is from an unknown person. Users are also willing to put all sorts of personal information in their posts and profiles. The problem is that many users are not too careful with their account settings and fail to ensure that they regularly check them. Identity thieves are adept at collecting information and images from accounts that are too open and where members freely give away information about themselves. Keep account settings tight, reviewing them regularly, post images that do not give too much information about the location or people in them. Ignore friend requests from people that are unknown to you – once they are a friend they have access to all information/images you make available.	4, 2
Chapter 9. Document production		
p. 69	Quick test: F, T, F, T, F, T	
p. 71	Quick test: F, T, F, T, T, F	
p. 73	Quick test: F, T, F, T, T, F, T	
Exam-style practice questions: download solutions at www.collins.co.uk/IGCSEICTrevision		
Chapter 10. Data analysis		
p. 77	Quick test: F, F, T, T, F, T	
p. 79	Quick test: T, F, F, T, F, T	
Exam-style practice questions: download solutions at www.collins.co.uk/IGCSEICTrevision		
Chapter 11. Presentations		
p. 83	Quick test: T, F, F, T, T, F	
p. 85	Quick test: F, F, T, T	
Exam-style practice questions: download solutions at www.collins.co.uk/IGCSEICTrevision		
Chapter 12. Data manipulation		
p. 89	Quick test: F, T, T, F, F, T	
p. 92	Quick test: T, F, T, F, T, F	
Exam-style practice questions: download solutions at www.collins.co.uk/IGCSEICTrevision		
Chapter 13. Web authoring		
p. 97	Quick test: F, T, F, F, T, T	
p. 101	Quick test: F, T, F, T, T, F	
Exam-style practice questions: download solutions at www.collins.co.uk/IGCSEICTrevision		